By Roger von Oech

A Whack on the Side of the Head

A Kick in the Seat of the Pants

Expect the Unexpected
(or You Won't Find It)

The Creative Contrarian

Creative Whack Pack

Innovative Whack Pack

Ball of Whacks

X-Ball

Y-Ball

Star-Ball

Rhombi

The **Creative Contrarian**

20 "Wise Fool" Strategies to Boost Creativity and Curb Groupthink

Roger von Oech

Illustrations by Bingo Barnes

WILEY

Published by John Wiley & Sons, Inc., Hoboken, New Jersey.

Published simultaneously in Canada.

Book design by Roger von Oech. Illustrated by Bingo Barnes.
Drawings on pages 103, 173, 177, and 191 by George Willett.
Drawings on pages 79–80 by Roger von Oech.

For general information on our other products and services or for technical support, please contact our Customer Care Department within the United States at (800) 762-2974, outside the United States at (317) 572-3993 or fax (317) 572-4002.

Wiley publishes in a variety of print and electronic formats and by print-on-demand. Some material included with standard print versions of this book may not be included in e-books or in print-on-demand. If this book refers to media such as a CD or DVD that is not included in the version you purchased, you may download this material at **http://booksupport.wiley. com.** For more information about Wiley products, visit **www.wiley.com.**

Library of Congress Cataloging-in-Publication Data:

Names: Von Oech, Roger, author.

Title: The creative contrarian : 20 "wise fool" strategies to boost your creativity and curb groupthink / Roger von Oech.

Description: First edition. | Hoboken, New Jersey : Wiley, 2021. | Includes bibliographical references and index.

Identifiers: LCCN 2021036604 (print) | LCCN 2021036605 (ebook) | ISBN 9781119843269 (hardback) | ISBN 9781119844716 (adobe pdf) | ISBN 9781119844709 (epub)

Subjects: LCSH: Creative ability.

Classification: LCC BF408 .V577 2021 (print) | LCC BF408 (ebook) | DDC 153.3/5--dc23

LC record available at https://lccn.loc.gov/2021036604

LC ebook record available at https://lccn.loc.gov/2021036605

Cover design: Paul McCarthy.
Cover image: © Getty Images | Miragec.
Printed in the United States of America
SKY10029410_082621

For:

Max, Axel, Vivian, and Lucy

May your Wise Fools shine now
and well into the future!

Contents

Introduction   1

Part I: Meet the Wise Fool   9

Part II: The Wise Fool Strategies   23

   1. Buck the Crowd 25

   2. Flex Your Risk Muscle 37

   3. Laugh at It 49

   4. Seek Other Right Answers 59

   5. Keep Playing with It 69

   6. Reverse Your Perspective 81

   7. Fool Around with the Constraints 91

   8. Build on an Odd Idea 99

   9. Look for Ambiguity 103

  10. See the Obvious 111

  11. Use Your Forgettery 117

  12. Drop What's Obsolete 125

  13. Kiss a Favorite Idea Goodbye 131

  14. Revisit a Discarded Idea 135

  15. Find What's out of Whack 139

16. Stop Fooling Yourself 145

17. Exercise Humility 153

18. Imagine the Unintended 159

19. Develop a Thick Skin 169

20. Shed an Illusion 173

Part III: Use Your Wise Fool Know-How   177

Selected Bibliography   193

Index of Proper Names   196

Acknowledgments   199

About the Author   200

Introduction

"If anyone among you thinks he is wise in this age, let him become a fool that he may become wise."

— St. Paul, *I Corinthians 3:18*

Discovery consists in looking at the same thing as everyone else and thinking something different.

— Albert Szent-Györgyi, Hungarian Biochemist

I've been a lifelong student of the creative process. From my college days on through to my professional career as an author, business consultant, speaker, conference producer, product developer, and more recently as a toy designer, I've been interested in how and when the mind does its best work.

When does my mind feel most alive? Truth be told, it's when I allow myself to take on the role of the Wise Fool. Indeed, I've had an enduring fascination with this character: his free-spirited energy, his unexpected observations, and most importantly, his ability to shake people out of their habitual responses to problems so that they might conjure up more imaginative solutions.

The Wise Fool is an archetypal figure — such as the Sage, the Magician, and the Healer — who resides deep within the human psyche and fulfills a purposeful role in society. The Wise Fool is the one who looks at life in different and often non-traditional ways and pushes back against the status quo. We might recognize this character today as *the creative contrarian.*

Historically, Wise Fools were hired by the powerful (kings, emperors, pharaohs) to be a kind of "thought pattern disrupter." Their job was to take a whack at the assumptions that kept their clients mired in conventional thinking. They did this so the rulers might see the issues before them in a fresh light.

When I don my Wise Fool's cap, I feel like I am in "my best thinking self." This means that I am a little less dogmatic and a lot more playful; less afraid to be the guy who asks the stupid questions and more skeptical of "received" truths; less convinced that I've got the right answer and more likely to see the humor in ambiguous situations. I'm also more amused at the unexpected and unintended things that come my way.

Decades ago, right after I completed my doctoral studies, I interviewed for a job with IBM (still the world's greatest company back then). To prepare myself, I read a history of IBM, and one particular passage jumped out at me. At a board meeting in the early 1960s, IBM chairman Tom Watson Jr. was discussing the company's culture, and he lamented that far too many IBMers thought alike, dressed alike, and behaved alike. "What we need here," he said, "are a few wild ducks." At my interview, I quoted this story (which delighted my interviewers), and told them that I wanted to be one of those "wild ducks" Watson desired. I got the job, but I soon realized that:

It's okay to be a wild duck just as long as you fly in formation.

From this, I learned that thinking in a different, contrary fashion wasn't always welcome. Fortunately, I listened to my inner Wise Fool, and decided to pivot. This experience showed me that there was a need for people to use their creative abilities and consider alternatives. Not all of the time obviously, but even just 5% of the day would be a real boon both to themselves and to their organizations. I filled this need by starting a company to help people develop their own creative thinking skills (which I brought to many organizations around the world).

During my many years of conducting creativity seminars in business, I discovered that those exercises I did that involved Wise Fool thinking were usually my clients' favorites. That's because they yielded a lot of provocative ideas pertaining to their respective companies. (The participants found that being a creative contrarian can be fun!)

Quick quiz: The term "Wise Fool thinking" may be foreign to some, but its underlying specifics are recognizable (and practiced) by many. For example, have you ever:

- Felt like you were in a room full of "crazy people" all thinking the exact same thing — and then mustered up the courage to offer a contrary viewpoint?

- Laughed at one of your most beloved ideas to test its validity?

- Felt dissatisfied with the first right answer you found, and then looked for some ambiguity in the problem to give yourself to room to think?

- Behaved counterintuitively to accomplish an objective, say, gone to the city to be alone?

If so, you're familiar with Wise Fool thinking.*

As I reflect on my life, I would say that having a measure of Wise Fool "savvy" has been an asset in my mental portfolio of skills, abilities, and beliefs. I'm not alone. Over the years, I have talked with successful people in various walks of life, and many of them have expressed a similar gratitude for having a bit of the Wise Fool in their outlook—especially when it was necessary to think differently, and then act contrary to the crowd to produce innovative ideas.

I believe that most people could benefit from having some Wise Fool know-how in their approach to the world. Unfortunately, there hasn't been a simple guidebook laying out the elements of Wise Fool thinking (sort of like what Machiavelli did for the ruthless management of power in *The Prince*, or

---

* **Important distinction:** There are two types of fools: the *Young Fool* and the *Wise Fool* (the subject of this work). The former often does stupid stuff, messes things up, and has neither the skills nor the understanding to know any better. The Wise Fool, on the other hand, does things by design—his objective is to challenge and provoke people's thinking into unfamiliar territory.

what Aristotle did for the essentials of dramatic theory in his *Poetics*).

That is, until now. I present to you: ***The Creative Contrarian: 20 "Wise Fool" Strategies to Boost Creativity and Curb Groupthink.*** This work provides you with the basics in how Wise Fools approach life, problem solving, decision making, and, of course, letting their voice be heard. In it, we will examine the 20 essential ideas that give Wise Fools their wisdom. These powerful Strategies will allow you to incorporate their cognitive orientation into your mental processes so that you too can do your own "best work."

Why did I write it? A quick story. A few years after starting my own company, I found myself in the office of Steve Jobs, then Apple's chairman — he was in his mid-20s, this was during his first stint at the company. We were talking about the ideas he would be presenting at an upcoming conference I was producing dealing with high-tech innovation. During our conservation, I asked him: "Why did you start Apple?" His answer has stayed with me ever since: "We make what we want for ourselves. I always wanted a personal computer, but there wasn't one available, so I had to put myself in a position to create one."

Similarly, I've long been infatuated with Wise Fools, and I wanted to create a guidebook that boiled their wisdom and strategies for being a creative contrarian into an easily accessible form. I also wanted to include some of my favorite stories in it — both from long ago and recent ones as well.

This is the sort of resource I wish had been available to me at various times in my own life, say, when I needed to think things over, and "unlearn" an idea or two — especially when I was making major life decisions. This also would have been a boost when I was planning projects, and certainly when I was in school (to counteract some of the dogmas that were being dished out).

This work is a modest "tip o' the cap" to the ancient Greek philosopher Socrates, history's most extraordinary Wise Fool. Socrates had, as you may recall, his own personal *daemon* — a kind of internal oracular spirit — to whom he could turn when he needed some guidance and inspiration. I contend that each of us has something similar nestled within our lobes: an inner creative contrarian with whom we can consult when we need to think differently or buck the crowd. Sometimes Wise Fools may say, "Kiss a favorite idea goodbye," or "Seek other right answers." At others, they may advocate, "Flex your risk muscle," or "Exercise humility." Whatever their counsel, it's prudent to give it consideration. Simply put, you may think of this book as:

A stimulant to help you gain a different perspective, and an antidote to conformity and groupthink.

You can read it all in one sitting if you wish. In putting it together, however, my primary design criterion has been to create a resource that you can dip into anywhere on a regular basis whenever you need a bit of inspiration from the Wise Fool to "think differently."

Some of you may be familiar with my products, perhaps one of my books, for example, *A Whack on the Side of the Head* (whose "Don't Be Foolish" chapter provided the seeds for this current work), or my creativity tools such as the *Creative Whack Pack* card deck (and app) and the *Ball of Whacks* line of design toys. If so, you are already aware of my fondness for the Wise Fool's contrarian behavior. You may also recognize a few of the anecdotes I've used to bring the Wise Fool to life. I trust these perennial ideas will continue to light up your mind and inspire your own Wise Fool!*

I hope you'll find **The Creative Contrarian** to be of value both when you need another point of view, and also when you're in groupthink situations and need to push back. I trust you will enjoy working and playing with the concepts in this book.

Stay curious and be imaginative!

Roger von Oech
Woodside, California

---

* You might be interested to know that I have been collecting Wise Fools of various sorts for over four decades: sculptures (in wood, steel, bronze, ceramic), drawings, etchings, posters, needlepoint, cups, jewelry, and masks. If you were to visit my studio, you would see Wise Fools just about everywhere!

Part I: Meet the Wise Fool

"Jesters do oft prove prophets."
— William Shakespeare, English Playwright

1. What Does the Wise Fool Do?

Let's suppose that you're dealing with a challenging issue and it resists your best efforts. You feel like you are doing every-thing "right" but things just aren't flowing. Perhaps your imag-ination is off or your powers of discernment aren't focused. You've tried various techniques to jump-start your creative process, but you still feel stuck. You think to yourself:

Who can give me a different perspective?

One answer is to do what problem solvers and decision makers since the dawn of civilization have done to stimulate their imaginations and improve their judgment:

Ask a Wise Fool what he thinks.

Wise Fools were consulted by Egyptian pharaohs and Baby-lonian kings. Their ideas were sought by Greek tyrants and Ro-man emperors. They advised Persian sultans, and also chiefs in the Pueblo, Hopi, and Sioux nations. They played an im-portant role at the courts of the Chinese emperors, and were prominently employed by European royalty in the Middle Ages and Renaissance.*

What did these Wise Fools do? Put very simply, it was their job to "whack" the king's thinking out of his habitual thought patterns. The king's advisers were often "yes-men" and syco-

---

* Both men and women can be Wise Fools: thinking like one has long been open to all! Historically, however, the majority of those who performed this role at court were males.

phants who told him exactly what he wanted to hear. The king
realized that this wasn't a good environment in which to make
decisions or conjure up promising alternatives. Therefore, he
gave his Wise Fool a *license to parody and ridicule* any proposal under discussion so as to shatter the conventional viewpoint
— in other words, to be a creative contrarian.

The Wise Fool's candid jokes and observations put the issue in a fresh light and forced the king to reexamine his assumptions. By listening to the Wise Fool, the king improved
his judgment, enhanced his creativity, and protected himself
from his groupthink milieu.

How do Wise Fools look at things? Well, they operate in
a world that runs counter to conventional patterns. Everyday ways of perceiving, understanding, and acting have little
meaning for them. They'll extol the trivial, trifle the exalted,

and parody the common perception of a situation. Here are some examples of the Wise Fool's contrarian approach to life:

Wise Fools are eager to challenge our usual perceptions. One might say, "If a man is sitting on a horse facing the rear, why do we assume that it is the man who is backwards and not the horse?"

They turn the rules on their head. They look at policies and think of reasons why the reverse objectives could also make sense. Many organizations espouse the value: "We Are Committed to Excellence." They say: "Let's shoot for mediocrity. Imagine the benefits: less product development time, lower training costs, less quality control, and less production time. If we had mediocre products, we'd have to learn how to sell more aggressively. I'm sure we would be successful because: *Nothing succeeds like mediocrity because everyone understands it so well.*"

Wise Fools are irreverent. One might pose a brain-teaser such as: "What is it that the rich man puts in his pocket that the poor man throws away?" When she answers, "Snot," she forces us to reconsider the wisdom of some of our most basic hygenic practices.

They can be absurd. Having lost his donkey, a Wise Fool knelt down and began exuberantly praising God. A passerby saw him and asked, "Your donkey is missing; why are you expressing your gratitude to the Almighty?" He replied, "I'm thanking Him for seeing to it that I wasn't aboard him at the time. Otherwise, I would be missing as well."

They ask odd questions. "If you put a dozen roses in your refrigerator and the next day they start smelling like Roquefort cheese, does the cheese smell like roses?"

They are paradoxical. "When I came home, I expected a surprise but there was no surprise for me, so, of course, I was surprised" (Wittgenstein); "All of the true things I'm about to tell you are shameless lies" (Vonnegut); "Only the ephemeral is of lasting value" (Ionesco).

Wise Fools observe the things most people overlook. "Why do people who pour cream into their coffee do so after the coffee is already in the cup, rather than pouring it in first and saving themselves the trouble of stirring?"

They can be cryptic. One might say that the best way to see something is with your ears. This may seem odd, but after you've thought about it, you might agree that *listening* to a well-written story or poem can stimulate your imagination more than *watching* TV or a video.

Many Wise Fools see life as a series of metaphors.
If a one took an intelligence test with this question on
it: "Which is true? A) Birds eat seeds, or B) Seeds eat
birds," she would answer both "A" and "B" because
she's seen dead birds decomposing on the ground "feeding" freshly fallen seeds.

Wise Fools can provoke us into thinking, perceiving, and
acting differently:

- Their offbeat comments can force us to focus on
  information that we had previously thought was
  irrrevelant.

- Their playful barbs might inspire us to conjure up
  an offbeat hypothesis, or perhaps jettison an obsolete assumption.

- Their candid statements of the obvious might force
  us to toss aside some of our arrogance.

- Their sobering directness might help us honestly
  assess the obstacles we could expect to encounter
  while implementing a new idea.

In other words, the Wise Fool is the character who jars us into an awareness that there are other ways to look at what we're doing, and that we should be seeking better answers than the ones we currently have. The great Danish physicist Niels Bohr felt that being a creative contrarian was a good way to come up with breakthrough ideas. During a tense brainstorming session, he told a colleague:

We all know your idea is crazy. The question is, whether it is crazy enough.

Some people, however, regard the Wise Fool as a simpleton, a dunce "whose elevator doesn't go all the way to the top," the imbecile "whose belt doesn't go through all the loops," the idiot "whose bell has no clapper," or the moron "who's a few French fries short of a Happy Meal."

Nothing could be further from the truth! It takes intelligence, imagination, cleverness, and insight to play the role of the Wise Fool. A good Wise Fool needs to be part actor and part poet, part philosopher and part psychologist. Because of their ability to open up people's thinking, Wise Fools in some cultures have been held in as much esteem as the priest, the medicine man, and the shaman.

The great benefit of the Wise Fool's antics and observations is that they stimulate our thinking. They jolt us in the same way that a splash of cold water awakens us when we're drowsy. We may not like their ideas. Some of them may irritate us and strike us as silly or useless. But they force us to entertain — perhaps only momentarily — alternative ways of looking at our situation.

2. Put on Your Wise Fool's Cap

So far, we have established that it's good to have a Wise Fool to consult with from time to time when we need a creative spark. But what do you do if there isn't one handy to help you put things into perspective? The answer is simple:

Be your own Wise Fool.

You're smart, right? Got a sense of humor? Capable of looking at things in a variety of ways? Then put on your Wise Fool's cap and dig into your bag of tricks. It will open your mind and clear your judgment. For example, try some of the following: laugh at the problem — perhaps ridiculing your basic assumptions. Point out the hypocrisy in a current situation. See the benefits of looking at it backwards. Doubt the things that others take for granted. Highlight the ambiguity in the problem.

Remember those occasions when you thought like a Wise Fool? Were you more creative? Did you generate a lot of different ideas? Were you bolder and less risk-averse? Were things more enjoyable? I bet the answer to most (if not all) of these questions is "yes." From my own 35-year experience conducting creativity workshops, I've found the best sessions I led were those where the participants allowed themselves *to be their own Wise Fools.*

A good analogy for Wise Fool thinking is to compare your mind to the transmission of a car. Most of the gears — first, second, drive, etc. — are designed to go forward, and to get you where you want to go. But sometimes, when you're stuck and can't make forward progress, you need to put the car in *reverse* so that you can back up and then go forward anew. Obviously you wouldn't want to drive in reverse most of the time, but it is an important gear to have in the appropriate circumstances.

Similarly, most of our thinking habits and strategies are employed to move ahead and to get things done. But sometimes, when you're stuck on a problem, you need to be able to back out of the current situation and then go forward in a different direction. That is what the Wise Fool is all about: **thinking like one is your mind's reverse gear!** And like the car's reverse gear, you probably don't need to adopt a Wise Fool mindset more than about 5% of the time.

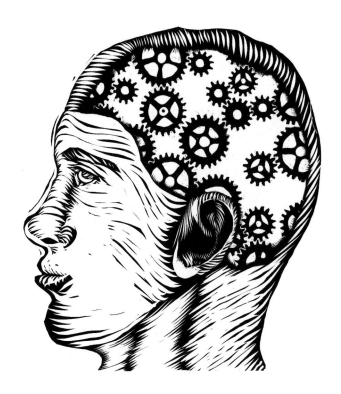

Thinking like a Wise Fool may not give you the right answer or solve your problem, but it will get you out of the rut you're in and put your thinking on a different mental path where you might find some better solutions.

Playing the Wise Fool is not only a lot of fun, it is also a good way to examine your most basic assumptions. Sometimes you'll discard a belief after the Wise Fool's scrutiny. But it can also happen that if the assumption can withstand a Wise Fool's probing, you'll have a much better appreciation for why you held that belief in the first place.

3. The Wise Fool Strategies

How easy is it to be your own Wise Fool? For some of us, the answer is: "Simple—it's as natural as breathing. I just flip a switch, and I'm there bucking the crowd." Many of us, though, have a bit more difficulty achieving this frame of mind. Since thinking like a Wise Fool and being a creative contrarian run counter to the conventional ways we have learned how to do things, we may need some assistance to think in this manner.

Allow me to introduce the "Wise Fool Strategies." These are ideas that will provide you with your Wise Fool know-how! For years, I've been curious about how Wise Fools perceive reality and operate in the world. I've especially wanted to discover the basic elements of their behavior so that anyone wishing to emulate them could do so.

To this end, I've explored my own thinking tendencies, and also shared ideas with other people who have the ability to tap into their own inner Wise Fools. In addition, I've stud-

ied the works of many scientists, artists, and writers looking for clues into what they had noticed in their own creative processes—especially when they had gotten a fresh perspective by engaging in Wise Fool behaviors. I've found that when people are thinking like creative contrarians, they:

- Use humor as a fun way to generate ideas
- Seek out alternative right answers
- Are reluctant to conform to the majority viewpoint
- Believe play is a mental lubricant
- Experiment with making up their own rules
- Like to mock pet ideas
- Possess the courage to stick their necks out

Based on my study, I have selected 20 Strategies that Wise Fools employ when they work through a problem, deliberate on a decision, or just want to do things differently. They are listed on page 21. You'll notice that each one sounds like it's a remark a Wise Fool might share with you if you asked one for their counsel. When you read the Strategies from first to last, you'll see that they offer three different types of advice: *contrary, creative, and cautionary:*

Contrary: the early ones deal with how Wise Fools break out of "groupthink" situations and express what's on their minds;

Creative: the middle ones provide a mix of problem-solving heuristics and creativity tips; and,

Cautionary: the later ones reflect their warnings in an unpredictable world.

Together, these 20 Strategies form a compendium of Wise Fool thinking. To develop your ability to think like a "creative contrarian," I highly recommend consulting them. Not only will these Strategies provoke different and original thoughts each time you turn to them, they will also become trusted companions whose guidance you will welcome!

4. Reap the Wise Fool's Bounty

In the next section, "Part II: The Wise Fool Strategies," I will bring these ideas to life by sharing stories and examples. I'll also discuss how you can benefit from including them in your cognitive repertoire. Read through them to get a sense

1. Buck the Crowd

2. Flex Your Risk Muscle

3. Laugh at It

4. Seek Other Right Answers

5. Keep Playing with It

6. Reverse Your Perspective

7. Fool Around with the Constraints

8. Build on an Odd Idea

9. Look for Ambiguity

10. See the Obvious

11. Use Your Forgettery

12. Drop What's Obsolete

13. Kiss a Favorite Idea Goodbye

14. Revisit a Discarded Idea

15. Find What's out of Whack

16. Stop Fooling Yourself

17. Exercise Humility

18. Imagine the Unintended

19. Develop a Thick Skin

20. Shed an Illusion

of what it's like to inhabit the Wise Fool's world. As you work with the Strategies, I encourage you to pay special attention to those that make you say:

Yes, that rings true for me!

Equally important, notice the ones that seem *distant from your experience* or that you disagree with. This latter group can be especially revealing — if you spend the time thinking about them. I know that when I allow myself to lower my resistance to those ideas that I typically dismiss as irrelevant or unattractive, I find that they can become doorways to answers I've been overlooking. I'm sure that different ones will speak to you, and that you will have fun determining which Strategies will become your personal favorites!

One of my preferred ways to use the Wise Fool Strategies is to consult them as an oracle. I like to go to them when I have a specific problem that I want to think more deeply about. Indeed, using them as an oracle is a fun and powerful application of the Wise Fool's wisdom. If you would like to do that now (and why not?), go to "Ask the Wise Fool Oracle" on page 178. That section provides you with in-depth instructions on how to use the Wise Fool in this fashion.

Have fun working with these ideas!

Part II:
The Wise Fool
Strategies

Buck the Crowd

**"Whenever you find yourself
on the side of the majority,
it is time to pause and reflect."**

— Mark Twain, American Writer

Humans like to flock! Why? Being surrounded by like-minded people is reassuring and pleasurable. It can also make us feel safe and provide a sense of well-being.

Wise Fools, however, know that following the herd is a poor way to get a clear picture of what is truly going on. They say it's important to pay attention to your own thoughts and observations rather than caving into group pressures. Indeed, they believe it is a good strategy to be a contrarian and go against the grain. This means taking time to look for the drawbacks in the majority opinion and to find the merits and possibilities in the minority one.

Most of us, though, follow the crowd for much of what we do. This was captured countless times in the classic television program, Allen Funt's *Candid Camera*, a show where concealed cameras filmed ordinary people in familiar yet unexpected situations. One of my favorite episodes has a woman waiting patiently for an elevator in an office building. After a few moments, the elevator arrives and the doors open. As she looks in, she sees that everyone is turned around, facing the rear of the elevator. She's a bit confused at first, but she quickly figures that the other people must know something she doesn't, and so, she, too, gets into the elevator and faces the rear! This scene is repeated with other "victims" who also face the rear. These scenes confirm what a lot of life teaches us:

The best way to get along is to go along.

Think about it: we are all subject to group pressures. If you examine your own behavior, you'll see how much you conform to the situations you encounter on a daily basis. Let's suppose that you're a pedestrian standing at the corner of an intersec-

tion in a big city. Eight or ten other people are also standing there with you. The "DON'T WALK" sign is flashing but no traffic is coming. Then one of the pedestrians ignores the sign and crosses the street against the light. And then another goes, and then another. In no time, all the other people have crossed the street against the light. And you do too, because you would feel really stupid being the only person still standing there.

Without conformity, the fabric of society would come apart. One of the costs we pay for the many benefits of our social existence is a piece of our own individuality. There are thousands of rituals we go through where our behavior must conform to the people around us — everything from the correct pronunciation of the words we speak to how close we can get to other people when we are speaking to them. If you don't conform, you might disrupt the flow of the everyday routines happening around you.

I got a serious lesson in conforming to standards by working as a machinist on a production line in a defense factory. I ran a high-speed drill press making pinhead-sized holes in thumb-sized blocks of military-grade steel. Several milling procedures after mine ultimately turned these components into bomb triggers. The holes I made had to be drilled in *exactly the right locations every single time.* The consequences for nonconformance were sobering: either an expensive piece of waste, or worse, a faulty bomb trigger with the potential to detonate prematurely. My supervisor was ever-vigilant about my work. And so was I!

Conformity has another benefit: in those circumstances where we don't know our way around, what do we do? That's right! We look to others for the right way to act. Suppose you're in a gym that's new to you, and not sure how to use a particular piece of equipment. What do you do? Probably look over to the person next to you and try the same approach she is using.

My favorite conformity story is about the 4th-century AD Christian philosopher St. Augustine. As a young priest in Milan, Augustine went to his bishop, Ambrose, for help with the following issue. Augustine was planning to spend a few months in Rome. His problem was that in Rome it was customary to celebrate the Sabbath on Sunday, while in Milan it was celebrated on Saturday. Augustine was confused as to which was the right day. Ambrose solved Augustine's problem by telling him:

When in Rome, do as the Romans do.

The Wise Fool says this is not bad advice when applied in moderation. There can be a dark side, however, to excessive conformity, especially when it's forced on those who have non-conforming views. A frightening depiction of this is Don Siegel's 1956 film, *The Invasion of the Body Snatchers* (based on a science-fiction novel by Jack Finney). This work has long been regarded in popular culture as a cautionary tale of the dangers of coercing everyone to think in the same way.

The plot: Alien seeds fall from the sky, landing in a farmer's field in the small California town of Santa Mira. The seeds then grow into plant-like pods, and inside them grow humanoids that take on the memories and outward appearances of the neighborhood's real humans. When the humans go to sleep, the "pod people" take over their bodies. The pod people repeat this process by growing new pods and transforming *their* neighbors. Thus, the population of pod people grows quickly. The pod people look just like the real humans they've copied except for one noticeable difference: their personalities seem "flat."

The film's protaganist is Miles Bennell, the town's doctor. Many of his patients have recently complained that their loved ones appear to have been replaced by "emotionless impostors." Miles then runs into an old flame, Becky Driscoll, and they chat about how the people of Santa Mira seem changed in many, small ways. As things progress, Miles and Becky finally figure out what's going on. But there's a danger: they're among the very few who haven't been transformed. Unfortunately for them, the majority will not leave them alone.

The leader of the town's pod people community is Dan Kauffman, a psychiatrist. He goes to Miles's office to encourage him and Becky to take a "brief sleep" so that they, too, can awaken and join the ranks of the transformed. Kauffman explains to Miles the virtues of living in a society without human emotion—it's an "untroubled world." He says that if everyone were like them, there would be no conflict, no disharmony, and no hate. It's wonderful when everyone is the same: no love, no desire, no ambition, and no faith. To Miles, this is a recipe for stultifying conformity, and he tells Kauffman he wants no part of it. To which Kauffman replies:

You have no choice.

At the film's climax, Miles and Becky escape from his office, and venture out on to the town's main thoroughfare, where they are forced to walk among the "new breed." To pass as a pod couple, they need to be emotionless and expressionless. As Miles warns Becky: "Show no interest or excitement." In other words, don't let anyone know what you're really thinking or feeling.

And then! A dog runs into the street in front of a speeding truck. Becky has a basic human reaction: she screams in horror. By doing so, she betrays herself and Miles. The pod people recognize that they're humans, and turn into a vicious mob bent on tracking down and destroying them. So much for nonconforming opinions in Santa Mira's brave new world! The enforcers will silence them.

Of course, new ideas and novel solutions—not to mention good decisions—are not born in a conforming environment. Whenever people get together, there is the danger of "groupthink." This is the phenomenon in which members of a group are more interested in getting the approval of other group members than in trying to generate innovative solutions to the problems at hand.

There is a delightful groupthink story about Alfred Sloan, the visionary chairman of General Motors. An idea was proposed at a board meeting he was leading, and everybody became excited about it. People said things like, "This will be highly profitable," "We'll smash the competition with this," and "Let's get it done as soon as possible."

After more discourse, Sloan said, "Let's vote on it." As the vote went around the table, each board member voted "Yes" on the proposal. When the vote came back to Sloan, he said, "I, too, vote 'Yes' and that makes it unanimous. For that reason, I'm going to table the motion until next month. I don't like what's happening to our thinking. We are looking at this idea from just one angle, and this is a poor way to make decisions. Therefore, I want everyone to spend the next 30 days examining this proposal from several different points of view." Sloan obviously understood that:

When everyone thinks alike, no one is doing very much thinking.

A month later at the next board meeting, the proposal was brought up again. This time it was voted down. Provided with an opportunity to break through the effects of groupthink, the members had come up with alternatives.

We find groupthink (and its sibling, the "herd mentality") everywhere: music, art, entertainment, fashion, education, politics, and, of course, investing. I remember one time visiting my cousin, a North Dakota farmer. He showed me a newly constructed pig cellar for breeding pigs. It was gorgeous! I asked him if he was happy with his new investment. He answered, "I would be except that the building inspector told me that everywhere he goes he sees people installing pig cellars. In eighteen months there will be a glut, and prices will go down." He was right: a year and a half later, prices for his pork products plummeted.

Perhaps the most famous example of the herd mentality was in Holland in 1634–1636 in which a sizable chunk of the normally sober-minded Dutch population fell into the grip of "Tulipmania"—the rage to own and invest in tulips. As the craze played out, prices for tulips — especially rare species — reached dizzying heights as people from all walks of life sold their possessions to procure the capital to speculate on tulip bulb futures. This frenzied gamble to "get rich quick" ended badly for those involved as tulip prices collapsed significantly faster than they had risen, and many people went bankrupt.

Along these lines, Edwin Nourse, who had a long career studying agricultural economics before becoming the first chairman of the (U.S.) Council of Economic Advisors, had this pertinent warning:

When all the forecasters agree, that's the time to watch out.

Scottish journalist Charles Mackay, an early student of mass psychology, investigated groupthink in its many forms: bubbles, manias, mobs, hysterias, and crusades. Summing up his ideas in his book *Extraordinary Popular Delusions and the Madness of Crowds* in 1841, Mackay observed: "People go mad in herds, while they only recover their senses slowly, and one by one."

Investor John Templeton, the man *Money* magazine called "the most successful global stock picker of the 20th century," had a deep, intuitive sense of large group behavior. He was also fortunate to own a strong contrarian streak. He provided this explanation of his investment philosophy: "Bull markets are born in pessimism, grow on skepticism, mature on optimism, and die in euphoria. The time of maximum pessimism is the best time to buy, and the time of maximum optimisn is the time to sell. If you want to have a better performance than the crowd, *you must do things differently than the crowd.*"

What does the Wise Fool recommend to combat the herd mentality? At the beginning of this section, I quoted Mark Twain's advice to consider alternatives when you find yourself in agreement with the majority. The Wise Fool would go one step further and say "Buck the crowd" and adopt the contrarian's policy of:

When everyone zigs, it's time to zag.

Here's an example of a person who "zagged." In August 1969, a few days after the Beatles' penultimate studio album had been recorded, the project was still without a name. The "Fab Four" and a few close advisors got together to brainstorm album titles. The prospective names they kicked around tilted toward the grandiose, and soon they played with calling the new album "Everest" in recognition of their towering contribution to the 1960s music scene. Of course, such a name would necessitate an expensive 10,000-mile weeklong photo shoot to the Himalayas (such things were done by successful rock stars back then). But at this point in the group's career, the Beatles were on the verge of disbanding and had little energy for such a trip.

What to do? Rock historian Ken McNab relates that drummer Ringo Starr, probably the most grounded of the musicians, reversed everyone's perception on the album name by suggesting: "Why don't the four of us just go out in front of the EMI recording studio and stroll across the 'zebra' crosswalk, and call the effort 'Abbey Road'?" Why not indeed! This simple solution took two hours to set up and shoot, and became the Beatles' most iconic photo. *Abbey Road* went on to become their biggest selling album.

As a way to sharpen your thinking (and also jettison obsolete assumptions), the Wise Fool recommends disagreeing with people whose ideas and beliefs are similar to your own opinions. Indeed, you may find that the opposite viewpoint makes more sense.

If you don't have anyone handy to disagree with you, why not take the contrary position on conventional wisdom. For example, here the Wise Fool challenges the validity of two well-known proverbs:

Don't put all of your eggs in one basket. The Wise Fool: "There are times when you have to *go all in* to motivate yourself and to get rid of excuses. There's an apocryphal story that when the Spanish conquistador Hernán Cortés landed at Veracruz, Mexico, in 1519 to take on the Aztec empire, the first thing he did after unloading his men and his equipment was to sink his ships. Then he told his men: 'You can either fight or you can die.' Sinking his ships removed a third alternative: giving up and returning to Spain."

A chain is no stronger than its weakest link. The Wise Fool: "Weak links are great! Many systems have weak links designed right into them. They're called 'fuses.' When a system gets overloaded, the fuse blows and saves the rest of the system from breaking down. After all, which part do you want to have damaged: the $100,000 one or the 10¢ one?"

Bucking customary perceptual habits can also be a good way for discovering the humorous side of things. A fun example is Till Eulenspiegel, the 14th-century German peasant trickster whose merry pranks were the source of numerous folk and literary tales. One day when Till was hiking in the mountains, he was seen to be crying while walking downhill and laughing merrily while climbing up. When asked the reason for his odd behavior, Till replied, "While going downhill I'm thinking of the strenuous climb up ahead and that makes me sad; and while hiking uphill, I'm anticipating the pleasure of the easy descent."

Wise Fools believe that if you can train your mind to think in a manner contrary to the herd, you will be right more than wrong. Much of this book is about their efforts to "zag," that is, discover alternative viewpoints. They will eliminate obsolete ideas, reverse their perspectives, muse over random information, forget limiting assumptions, piggyback on strange ideas, seek out ambiguity, imagine unintended consequences, flex their risk muscles to go after "sacred cows," and laugh at the status quo.

Summary: The Wise Fool says that in those situations where you find yourself agreeing with the people around you, a prudent strategy is to stand back and ask, "What am I not seeing here? What's the downside to this approach? What alternative points of view should I be giving more credence to?"

One more thought for bucking the crowd: In his charmingly pugnacious book, *Letters to a Young Contrarian*, the British iconoclast Christopher Hitchens urged this simple caution for maintaining your independence: "Don't allow your thinking to be done for you by any party or faction, however high-minded. Distrust any speaker who talks confidently about 'we,' or speaks in the name of 'us.' Distrust yourself if you hear these tones creeping into your own voice." Good advice? You be the judge!

Flex Your
Risk Muscle

"If the Creator had a purpose in equipping us with a neck, He surely meant for us to stick it out."

— Arthur Koestler, Hungarian/British Writer

The nail that sticks up
will be hammered down.
— Japanese Proverb

It takes courage to buck the crowd. If you're overly concerned with other people's opinions, you'll have difficulty expressing unusual viewpoints or making the offbeat remarks that fuel further discussion. Wise Fools believe that everyone has a "risk muscle." One way to keep it in shape is by speaking candid truths. It is by flexing their risk muscles that Wise Fools perform their chief role as "conformity busters" in groupthink situations. Their contrary ideas can lead to more creative solutions. Let's take a closer look.

The classic study of conformity was done by psychologist Solomon Asch in the 1950s. Asch's objective was to determine how easily a test subject would alter his judgment to conform with a group. Here is the setup. A subject was told he was taking a "vision test" and asked to match lines on two different cards. The first card had a single vertical line on it, and the second had three vertical lines, one of which was the same length as the line on the first card and the other two lines were noticeably either longer or shorter.

Here's the experiment's intriguing part: the subject sat at a table with five other "participants," who were, unbeknownst to him, confederates of Asch and had been instructed to give the same wrong answer to each trial. One by one, each of the confederates gave his incorrect answer. Then it was the test subject's turn to state what he thought was the correct answer. Would he conform to the group's wrong answer, or would he give his own independent correct answer? The results were startling: at one time or another about 75% of the subjects conformed with the group's incorrect answer, and nearly 40% of all the trials resulted in incorrect answers.

The kicker — at least from the Wise Fool's perspective — is that Asch did a variation on the experiment in which he instructed one of his five confederates to give a correct answer prior to the test subject's choice. When this happened, the test subject's rate of conformity fell to less than 5%. Because the prevailing groupthink mindset had been broken, the subject felt free to speak candidly and provide what he thought was the true answer.

In other words, just one dissenting voice from the otherwise unanimous group had the benefit of producing more diverse opinions and thus curbing groupthink. This is one of the most valuable functions that Wise Fools perform! Indeed, if you've ever been at a gathering where all the other people agreed on a single viewpoint (different from yours) and were tempted to hold your tongue, then I'm sure you were grateful to the person who objected to what was happening, and provided you with the backbone to say what you were really thinking. The Wise Fool encourages you to provide this service to other people as well. Flexing your risk muscle allows you to speak up and say what is on your mind — a key ingredient for success, in the Wise Fool's opinion. As the American comedienne Joan Rivers put it:

I have succeeded by saying what everyone else is thinking.

This insight could be the motto for Wise Fools everywhere. It is their job, after all, to be candid. Indeed, sometimes they are the only people brave enough to give voice to what's on everyone's minds (but afraid to discuss). This is a very positive thing.

The Wise Fool is often the one entrusted to point out the proverbial "elephant in the room." You're familiar with this beast: it's the obvious problem or controversial issue that people avoid talking about because it is uncomfortable to do so. For example, many families have difficulty resolving a troubling situation because they find it unpleasant to bring up the "elephant" of, say, a member's alcohol, drug, or gambling addiction. Discussing this subject can be painful, but since the "elephant" is usually the root cause of the problems the family is facing, there can be no progress made until it is addressed. The Wise Fool's candor is invaluable here.

Every organization has its share of "elephants" as well. Meetings and problem-solving sessions can be unproductive if participants are uncomfortable discussing an associate's hid-

den agenda, a leader's suffocating egotism, or a colleague's habitual lack of follow-through. Again, having a Wise Fool present to articulate these things as stumbling blocks can make the sessions more successful.

Sometimes people don't speak up because the consequences can be *professionally or politically costly*. A wonderful example is the classic Hans Christian Andersen children's story "The Emperor's New Clothes." Here is a quick summary.

A vain, clothes-loving Emperor hires two tailors to sew him a beautiful suit. The tailors, who are actually con men, say the suit's fabric is endowed with an unusual property—the material is invisible to anyone who is incompetent or stupid. This special property appeals to the Emperor: he reckons he can use it to weed out the undesirables in his realm.

While the suit is being "made," the Emperor sends his ministers to monitor the tailors' progress. Because they are afraid of looking incompetent, the ministers report back that the work is "marvelous" even though they haven't actually seen the fabric. Finally, the tailors tell the Emperor the suit is finished, and they mime dressing him in his glorious new garments.

The Emperor then marches in a procession before his subjects. Of course, he beams at the reception his new wardrobe receives. That's because while the suit was being made, the townspeople had been fed stories about the fabric's unique properties, so they—not wanting to appear stupid or incompetent—play along and shout out their "oohs" of admiration for the suit's beauty. No one is brave enough to admit to what he is actually seeing: a middle-aged man walking down the street naked. At this point, a child in the crowd, too young to understand the pretense, blurts out:

The Emperor isn't
wearing any clothes!

Like a pin bursting a balloon, the youngster's candid comment dispels the charade, and the townspeople feel free to acknowledge what they had actually been seeing but had previously lacked the courage to state publicly.

The townspeople quickly understand that their perceptions had been correct, but that their ability to be frank had been overruled by their survival instincts. Think of the cognitive dissonance they were experiencing!

The Wise Fool says an important time to flex your risk muscle is when you're dealing with "sacred cows." Sacred cows are "forbidden-to-question" assertions and beliefs, and they are especially mind-clouding when they are derived from an exalted authority.

For example, 2,400 years ago, the great philosopher Plato put forth the idea that the circle was the perfect shape for celestial movement. For the next two millennia, astronomers believed that planetary orbits were circular — even though their observations didn't jibe with that Platonic assertion. Even Copernicus proposed circular orbits in his heliocentric model of the universe. Only after much soul-searching did the 17th-century German mathematician Johannes Kepler summon the nerve to question the circle's primacy — astronomy's long-standing sacred cow — and posit that each planet's orbit is actually an ellipse. The Wise Fool would say that by flexing his risk muscle Kepler "deviated away from the realm of authorized ideas" to create a solution that successfully explained planetary movement!

Have you ever censored yourself because you felt your line of inquiry ran contrary to the prevailing dogma relating to that issue? Of course, everyone has! That's because there are "received truths" in all spheres of human activity. Sometimes the sacred cows are called "settled science," and sometimes they are the "party line," or the "dominant paradigm."

If your Wise Fool is on active duty, your job is to challenge the sacred cows you confront—and then explore what can be discovered by ignoring them. Remember: If you don't question them, entire families of divergent solutions will remain hidden from you. Here are two examples, one from religion and one from the military, of individuals who successfully used this strategy.

Appalled by the Roman Catholic Church's lucrative business of selling indulgences to sinners wishing to shorten their time in purgatory, the 16th-century German priest Martin

Luther used his extensive knowledge of Greek, Latin, and Hebrew to examine the Biblical source materials and question the basic tenets of Church dogma. He found there was no theological justification for selling indulgences. He concluded that God's grace alone was sufficient for one's personal salvation, and not the machinations of the Church hierarchy.

After Luther made his position public in 1517 by nailing his "95 Theses" to the door of Wittenberg church, he was then tried for heresy and excommunicated by Pope Leo X. The ensuing consequences of Luther's challenge of the indulgence sacred cow were significant: the Protestant Reformation (which created a "back-to-basics" personal version of Christiantity), and the Catholic Counter-Reformation (whose ecclesiastical housecleaning gave the Church a renewed vitality).

From the 1890s up to World War II, the battleship played the central role in naval strategic thinking about the best way to project power. Its hallowed status was due to its thick armor and big guns that could destroy an opponent's forces at distances of up to 20 miles away.

In the early 1920s, American General Billy Mitchell, an experienced World War I fighter pilot commander, lambasted this floating sacred cow by calling it a dinosaur, and stating that airpower would soon play the most important role in naval warfare. Mitchell even provided a live demonstration showing how planes could sink a battleship. He also advocated for the development of a new vessel, the aircraft carrier, to bring significantly more air power to naval combat.

Since the Army and Navy faced budget cutbacks at the time, Mitchell's views didn't play well with the military brass, who were busy protecting the status quo (an example of Upton Sinclair's truism: "It is difficult to get a man to understand something when his salary depends on his not understanding it"). After Mitchell's aviation ideas were ignored, he was quoted in newspapers nationwide as saying, "The General Staff knows as much about the air as a hog does about skating." Though supported by the public, Mitchell was soon hounded out of the Army after a bitter court-martial. Mitchell's challenge to military orthodoxy did bear fruit. In the late 1920s, as a cadre of his junior officers rose in the ranks, the War Department began modernizing its air capabilities.

Twenty years after Mitchell's original warning, the Japanese aerial attack on Pearl Harbor (made possible by their aircraft carriers) vindicated his vision of the kind of damage a combined sea and air assault could wreak. Six months later, at the epic Battle of Midway in 1942, naval vessels from both sides never came closer than 175 miles of one another because the attacks were carried out by aircraft. For his work promoting air power, Mitchell was posthumously awarded the Congressional Gold Medal in 1946.

Of course, there are many examples of where challenging the established order doesn't produce "happy" endings. An extreme one is *1984*, George Orwell's cautionary novel about a totalitarian government that has gone too far. In a closing scene, the book's protagonist, "thoughtcrime" suspect Winston Smith, is interrogated by Party enforcer O'Brien. (Winston's thoughtcrime consisted of daring to procur for himself an unauthorized pen and notebook and then writing down his personal thoughts, ideas like "I want to have the freedom to say such things as 2 + 2 = 4.")

O'Brien explains to Winston that his personal truths and perceptions are delusions, and that whatever he thinks is real must be surrendered to the Party's truth. Initially, Winston isn't afraid because he feels the authorities can never get inside his mind. He is then strapped to an electrical pain-dispensing machine.

O'Brien holds up the back of his hand to Winston with four fingers sticking up, and asks: "How many fingers am I holding up?" Winston replies "Four."

O'Brien then asks: "And if the Party says that it is not four but five — then how many?" Once again, Winston answers, "Four."

"There are five," O'Brien says, and administers another electrical jolt. The torture continues. At long last, Winston screams out, "Five, anything you like. Just stop the pain." Winston has surrendered to the Party's truth and its narrative of reality.

*   *   *

Finally, I would like to add a personal story about how I developed my own "risk muscle" when I was 11 years old. My 6th-grade teacher, Mr. Rodefer, taught me that being creative and being obnoxious are sometimes very similar, but that they are not the same thing. He showed me how to differentiate the two by giving me a license to try different things. We had an agreement: I'd run a lap around the schoolyard for every obnoxious act I committed, but he would reward me for my new ideas. This allowed me to take chances.

The result? Well, I did have to run some laps that year (actually 129 laps), but I also did some very creative things. The best part is that I learned how to stick my neck out. I have used this license ever since (and, yes, I still occasionally have to do the equivalent of running a lap around the schoolyard).

Five years after that, I began what became for me a serious avocation: hitchhiking. This arose out of: a) my reading Jack Kerouac's Beat-era novel, *On the Road*; b) my curiosity to go to places I had never been before; and, c) having very little money. From my midteens to my mid-20s, I hitchhiked over 30,000 miles, mainly in the United States and Canada, but also throughout Europe. It was quite an education! I got rides from a variety of different people: an Anglican vicar in England took me to have sherry with the writer John Betjeman (who shortly thereafter was named Poet Laureate of Britain);

an older man in Bavaria who told me stories about being a student in school in the late 1910s with Heinrich Himmler (who later founded the dreaded Nazi paramilitary *Schutzstaffel* or *SS*); a youth choir leader in British Columbia who described how she scored music for different voice groups; and a cowboy in Nevada who bootlegged pornography from California to Utah. Back then, people weren't afraid to pick up strangers and share stories from their lives.

Summary: The Wise Fool believes that everyone has a "risk muscle." You keep it in shape by trying new things and speaking candidly. An important part of thinking like a Wise Fool is taking a different viewpoint from the majority in order to prevent "groupthink" situations. Give yourself permission to express what's on your mind. As the Wise Fool puts it, "Somebody has to say it, and it might as well be you. Ask what 'elephants in the room' can you make visible? In what situations do you see the 'emperor' not wearing any clothing? Challenge a few sacred cows and see where that leads your thinking." You may discover new solutions that wouldn't otherwise be visible. What hallowed policies, dogmas, sacred cows, and esteemed models can you go after?

The Irish playwright Oscar Wilde once observed: "A man is least himself when he talks in his own person. Give him a mask, and he will tell you the truth." If you substitute a "Wise Fool license" for "mask," you get pretty much the same thing: the courage to "flex your risk muscle" and to be less concerned about the judgment of others, and the boldness to be different.

Wise Fool Strategy #3

Laugh at It

"As soon as you have made a thought, laugh at it."

— Lao Tzu, Chinese Philosopher

Humor is a favorite tool of Wise Fools. They believe that if you can laugh at something — be it a problem, the design of a work space, the plotline of a novel, or your relationship with another person — then you'll be more likely to think about it in a fresh way.

For example, one day a client of mine had a new product design team get into a really whacky mood, and so they decided to make fun of their product. They were zany, goofy, and off-the-wall. The meeting was a great success, and many new ideas were generated. The next week, everybody was in a more serious mood and no new ideas were generated. Moral: There's often a close relationship between the "aha" of discovery and the "ha-ha" of humor.

Indeed, the mental processes underlying humor — challenging assumptions, breaking set, putting ideas into unusual contexts, seeking ambiguity, combining different concepts, asking offbeat what-if questions, and making fun of the rules — are effective creative thinking techniques in their own right.

Why is this? First of all, humor puts you at ease. Do you feel more comfortable talking with someone who has just told you a joke or with someone who is deadly serious? Would you rather listen to a speaker who approaches her subject in a plodding manner or one who has just given you a lighthearted aside on the state of your business?

A humorous frame of mind not only loosens you up, it can also enhance your creativity. This has been shown in psychological tests delving into the role humor plays in stimulating a creative outlook. Here's an example of how the tests are structured. Typically, participants are divided into two equal groups. One group sits passively in a quiet room for half an hour prior to the test. The other group spends the same time in another room listening to recordings of standup comedians telling jokes like:

Question: How deep is the ocean?
Answer: Just a stone's throw.

Question: Why can't you hear a pterodactyl go to the bathroom?
Answer: The "P" is silent.

Question: What's the last thing you see when moles go into their holes?
Answer: Molasses.

Question: Why did the chicken go to the séance?
Answer: To get to the other side.

Report: I just read an interesting account about a 13th-century feudal uprising in France where a duke's son was killed by rebels who used a trebuchet to knock him off the battlements using the only available ordnance: a peasant's decapitated head. It was the first-recorded instance of a *serf-face-to-heir missile*.

Then both groups take the creativity test. The one that has been listening to the comedy usually does much better, not only in generating more ideas but also in the divergent ("off the beaten path") nature of these ideas. The psychologists reckon that the comedy loosens up their thinking and creates an environment where people can look at things in different ways.

Second, humor stretches your thinking. The term "just a stone's throw" typically indicates a short distance — perhaps 50 feet or so. But when you throw a rock into water, it travels until it reaches the bottom — perhaps as much as seven miles, depending on where you toss it. The punch line forces you to make a shift in how you think about a "stone's throw." Getting the joke then is an exercise in "breaking set" — one of the Wise Fool's prime objectives and also a key aspect of creative thinking. For if a stone's throw can mean seven miles, who is to stop you from looking at a broken light bulb as a *knife*, or driveway gravel in a shoebox as a *muscial instrument*?

Third, humor forces you to combine ideas that are usually not associated with one another. Few people think that "dinosaur urine" and "phonetics" have much in common. Yet for purposes of this joke, this unlikely duo is brought together into one concept. If such juxtapositions are possible, then why not try combining other unrelated ideas? How about globes and sandpaper, or swimming pools and onions?

Fourth, humor can be transgressive: it can encroach on the boundaries of what you think is socially acceptable or "what is proper." For example, the above "mole" joke is a tad naughty (at least that's the way it seemed to me in the context of when I first heard it). You "get" the joke when you understand the double meaning of molasses: it connotes a dark sugary liquid, and its homonym (*mole-asses*) is a cruder version of "rodents' rear ends."

For some people, this might violate their sense of good taste. (Of course, the playful nature of the joke mollifies the transgression. There are many significantly more offensive jokes out there, and one is free to accept them in the spirit in which they're offered, or reject them.) Hearing this joke, however, might put you in a mood to dispense with other formalities and social graces. Indeed, creativity often requires us to challenge our own norms. Ever tear a page out of an expensive art book to hang it on your wall? To some, that's a no-no because it destroys the book's integrity. How about taking a few cards from a brand-new card deck and putting them in the spokes of a kid's bicycle? The deck is now worthless for playing poker or solitaire, but the bike is certainly a lot more fun. How about urinating in the cabin of an airplane? That's a taboo, right? Well, there are more than a few stories from World War II up to the present time about pilots who were unable to lower their landing gear because of a loss of hydraulic fluid, and who then solved this problem by urinating into the hydraulic fluid reservoir to restore pressure.

Fifth, humor allows you to take things less seriously. In the "chicken-séance" joke, the field of spiritualism is mocked. The Wise Fool believes that if you can make fun of something, then you're more likely to challenge the rules that give that "something" its legitimacy, and perhaps think of alternatives.

And, finally: the "serf-face-to-heir missile" joke. It's a pun with a long setup—clever, but still a groaner. Indeed, it's shameless, and you have to have guts to tell a joke like that. But it imparts to its listeners a kind of fearlessness to entertain other seemingly "out there" possibilities. How about cosmological string theory that describes the universe in 11 dimensions? Why not? Let's see if we can think of a 12th one! Mixing together proteins from million-year-old DNA samples to create a "fountain of youth" elixir? Hey, what resources can I add to the mix? Let's shoot for immortality!

Humor is an effective tool with even the most serious of problems. As the physicist Niels Bohr put it:

There are some things so serious you have to laugh at them.

There are occasions when you have to laugh at what you're doing—if for no other reason than to clear out your mind. You're probably familiar with "Occam's Razor." (Named after the 14th-century English logician William of Ockham, it states that "in competing explanations, the simplest solution is most likely to be the right one.") Wise Fools have a "Razor" too! Theirs states that if you have a topic that doesn't allow you to laugh at or ridicule it,* then chances are that topic is too fragile to be thought about in any other way—seriously or otherwise.

Wise Fools know that humor may not solve your problem, but it can put you in a mood more conducive to do so. Some people, however, are so closely wed to their ideas that they put them up on a pedestal. It's challenging to be creative when you have so much ego tied up in an idea in the form in which it already exists. Thus, loosen up and consider the Wise Fool's credo:

It's not so important to be serious as it is to be serious about the important things.

The monkey wears an expression of seriousness that would do credit to any great scholar.

But the monkey is serious because he itches.

---

* Political polemicist Saul Alinksy: "Ridicule is your most potent weapon. It is almost impossible to counteract ridicule. Also, it infuriates the opposition, which then reacts to your advantage." (Rule #5 in his *Rules for Radicals*.)

From my own experience conducting creativity workshops, I have found that humor works wonders to stimulate the flow of ideas. If, early on in a session, I encourage the participants to be humorous in their dealings with the problem, their answers are usually more interesting and provocative. Not only that, they're also more candid in their approach to the more serious issues that I subsequently present to them. The corollary to this is that if I don't use humor near the beginning, the people are more likely to sit on their hands and be judgmental.

Here's one of my favorite exercises I use to loosen up my seminar participants' thinking: I have them make up humorous and irreverent mottos for their organizations and products. You might try this with your own issue. Here are some fun ones for you:

- The Walt Disney Company: "The place where 'when you wish upon a star,' we charge you for it."

- Microsoft: "We're arrogant and we should be."

- Bank of America: "Where you're not alone until you want a loan."

- The IRS: "Service is part of our name, but just remember it's the last part."

- Procter & Gamble: "Where innovation is acceptable just as long as it's been tried before."

- IBM: "Where creative people meet, and meet, and meet."

- Weyerhaeuser (forest products company): "We take a stand . . . and then cut it down."

- Hewlett-Packard: "At Hewlett-Packard there's a better way and it will be ready in two years."

- Kaiser Permanente Medical Group: "Good people, good medicine, good luck!"

- Intel: "We're a leader in technology whether the customer needs it or not."

- China: "Why should we be concerned with human rights when we have so many humans left?"

- Cisco: "We're the glue that holds your problems together."

- United Airlines: "Customer service is our #1 priority: please leave your complaint at the beep."

- AT&T: "We put the 'work' in networking."

- General Mills: "We're behind the customer every step of the way."

- Pfizer: "We've got the best drugs on 42nd Street."

- Stanford University: "In tuition we trust."

- American Potato Board: "For all you do, this spud's for you."

- Harrah's Casino: "You'll have a good time if you're lucky."

- National Education Association (a teacher's union): "Lean to the left. Lean to the left. Stand up! Sit down! Strike, strike, strike!"

- Accenture Consultants: "We're not only smarter than you are, we're also younger than you are."

- Kimberly-Clark (paper products company): "We've got a product for every hole in your body."

- Mountain Dew: "The only soft drink that comes out of your body the same color as it goes in."

- Apple: "If you wanted support you should have bought Jockey."

Advertising legend David Ogilvy would agree with this approach. As he put it: "The best ideas come as jokes. Your thinking needs to be as funny as possible." Indeed, one of the Wise Fool's central messages is that we should not take ourselves too seriously. German philosopher Friedrich Nietzsche took this idea to heart and wrote the following epigram:

I laugh at any master who lacks the grace to laugh at himself.

and then—in good-humor—had it inscribed over the door to his house!

The American journalist H.L. Mencken had a similar philosophy:

Human life is basically a comedy.
Even its tragedies often seem
comic to the spectator,
and not infrequently they
have comic touches to the victim.
Happiness consists largely in the
capacity to detect and relish them.
A man who can laugh, if only at
himself, is never really miserable.

This is something we all should keep in mind. Several years ago, I asked David Burge (the "Iowahawk" philosopher) about the current state of humor in our society. He replied: "Most generations laugh at what previous generations censored. The current generation censors what previous generations laughed at." Certainly something to think about.

Summary: The Wise Fool says: "Be a little whacky and ask what's funny about what you're doing. What can you make light of in this situation? What's particularly amusing? Be a little less serious. Let down your filter of what you consider to be 'stupid,' and roast some of your basic beliefs. For example, think of an important standard you use to measure ideas. What would be possible if you loosened that standard?" As the Austrian trickster logician Ludwig Wittgenstein put it:

"If people never did silly things, nothing
intelligent would ever get done."

Wise Fool Strategy #**4**

Seek Other Right Answers

**"Nothing is more dangerous
than an idea, when it's
the only one you have."**

— Émile-Auguste Chartier, French Philosopher

Wise Fools believe that if you have only one idea (solution, answer, perspective) of how something should be done, then you have only one course of action open to you. This is certainly a risky proposition in a world where flexibility is a vital survival skill. They operate as though there is always more than one right answer for any given problem, and it's important to look for alternatives.

One of my favorite stories about this happened when I was a sophomore in high school. My English teacher drew a chalk dot on the blackboard. She then asked the class to look at it and tell her what it was. A few moments passed, and no one volunteered. Finally, someone blurted out, "A chalk dot on the blackboard." After that, more silence. No one had anything to add.

"I'm astounded," the teacher told us. "I did a similar exercise yesterday with a group of six-year-olds, and they thought of many different things it could be: a wheel, a bird's eye, a marble, food stain on a shirt, cross-section of a banana, a bindi, rabbit poop, and so on. They had their imaginations going at full blast!"

In the 10-year span between kindergarten and high school, not only had we learned how to find the right answer, we had also lost some of the drive to seek out more than one right answer. We had learned how to be specific, but *we had lost a lot of our imaginative power.*

Seeking out just "one right answer" can have a grave consequence on the way we deal with problems. Most people don't like problems, and when they come across them, they often respond by taking the first way out they can find—even if they solve the wrong problem.

For example, the bandleader Count Basie once found himself in the following predicament with a nightclub owner. Basie had become frustrated because the club's piano was always out of tune, and he angrily told the owner, "I'm not coming back until you fix it." A month later, Basie got a call from the owner saying that everything was fine. When he came back, the piano was still out of tune. "You said you fixed it!" an angry Basie cried out. "I did," came the reply. "I had the piano painted." *
An amusing story, to be sure, but most of us encounter similar situations on at least a weekly basis.

Sufi educator Idries Shah captured the essence of this idea in the following *koan*-like statement:

A solved problem is as useful to the human mind as a broken sword on the battlefield.

Shah understood that broken swords aren't worthless: they

---

* The owner likely addressed most of his club's problems with decor-related solutions — it was his *modus operandi*. It's like the Abraham Maslow quip, "People who are only good with hammers tend to see every problem as a nail."

are better than no weapon at all. Similarly, past solutions can be also be useful — when applied judiciously. His point, however, is that the human mind's purpose is to challenge and to probe. Since people often stop looking for solutions once they've found one ("the battle is over"), a solved problem can hinder further mental engagement, even though that might be the best course of action.

I once did a series of creativity seminars for the senior staff of a large computer company. The president had asked me to come in because he was concerned about the "sluggish cognitive atmosphere" in the top ranks. When his people would make a proposal, that's all they would make — just one. They typically wouldn't present other options. Since most of them had been educated to look for the one right answer, they usually didn't go beyond the first one they found. The president understood that it was easier to make good decisions if he had a variety of proposals and ideas from which to select. He was also worried about how stodgy this "one-idea" habit had made their thinking. If someone were presenting only one idea, he or she would usually propose the "sure thing" rather than take a chance on a less likely, offbeat idea.

This situation fostered a poor climate for generating innovative ideas. Summoning up my own Wise Fool, I gave them the following advice:

Look for the second right answer.

Often, it is the second (or fourth or tenth) right answer, which, although strange or weird, is precisely what you need to solve a problem in an innovative way.

Sometimes the value of a second right answer is that it shows just how bad the first right answer really is. For example, economist Milton Friedman was driving along in postwar West Germany in the late 1940s and spotted a large group of workers shoveling out a building site. Curious about this, Friedman asked his German host, "Why don't you get a bulldozer and other mechanized equipment to do that job?" His host replied, "Ah, you don't understand—this provides jobs." Friedman, quick as always, responded, "Well, in that case, why don't you just give them some spoons!"

By exaggerating his solution to the excavation problem, Friedman highlighted the ridiculousness of the current approach, and in doing so, got those involved to consider other right answers.

A simple and effective technique for finding more answers is to change the way you ask questions. How many times have you heard someone ask, "What's the *answer*?" or "What's the *cause*?" These people are looking for *the* answer and *the* cause. And that's all they'll find — just one. The Wise Fool says that if you train yourself to ask questions that solicit plural answers — such as "what are the *answers*?" and "what are the *causes*?" — people will think a little more deeply and offer more than one idea.

Most human interactions are open to multiple interpretations — all depending on the motivations and perceptions of the people involved. One of the best film treatments of this idea is *Rashomon*, Akira Kurosawa's classic psychological thriller set in medieval Japan. The story focuses on the inves-

tigation of an apparent murder of a samurai who had been traveling in the forest with his wife. Viewers are then provided with four widely divergent accounts of the incident from the characters involved: a bandit, the samurai's wife, the dead samurai (told through a medium), and a woodcutter who had been at the scene.

Each witness has a different interpretation of the "truth," and what emerges is how contradictory and self-serving each of their versions is. In the end we're not quite sure whether the samurai's death was a murder, an accident, a suicide, or simply a dueling fatality. Since the film's release in 1950, the term "Rashomon effect" has entered into our language to describe the phenomenon whereby people have quite different accounts of the same event. Only by considering the situation from more than one perspective do we begin to understand what has happened.

Sometimes we get so locked into our routine ways of doing things that we need a little extra help to break free of the first right answer. Often, this motivation comes in the form of problems. The Wise Fool invites us to consider that when problems disrupt our routines, they offer the benefit of making us search for fresh answers and solutions.

A major form of disruption is failure. When things go smoothly, we don't think about them. But when they fail, it means the current approach isn't working and it's time to find a new one. Indeed,

Most people don't change when they "see the light." They change when they "feel the heat."

A friend who had been fired from a job told me: "Yeah, getting fired was really traumatic, but it turned out to be the best thing that ever happened to me. It forced me to come to grips with who I was as a person. I had to look at my strengths and weaknesses with no delusions at all. It forced me to get out and scramble. Six months later, I was in a much better situation."

This same disruption principle is evident at large companies, institutions, and organizations. For example, after the supertanker *Exxon Valdez* broke open off of Alaska in 1989, thereby polluting the coast with millions of gallons of oil, the petroleum industry was forced to rethink and toughen up many of its safety standards regarding petroleum transport. The disintegration of the *Challenger* (1986) and *Columbia* (2003) space shuttles caused a similar thing to happen at NASA. The sinking of the *Titanic* (1912) led to the creation of the International Ice Patrol, and legally mandated iceberg reporting. The September 11, 2001, terrorist attack on the *World Trade Center* forced architects to significantly raise their fire retardation standards in new high-rise building construction. The catastrophic 2004 Indian Ocean Tsunami forced world seismic monitoring authorities to change how they disseminate and share warning information. The coronavirus pandemic of the early 2020s forced many institutions and businesses to change where, when, and how their employees worked, and also how they dealt with their customers.

The history of discovery and invention is filled with people whose routines were interrupted and who were forced to come up with "second right answers" and alternative solutions. An important example of this phenomenon is the search for pepper. From the Middle Ages on, pepper was the most important spice traded between Europe and the Far East. That's because no other spice except pepper made heavily salted meat edible, and in Europe no form of preservation other than salting was generally employed. Thus, it was salt and pepper that stood between meat-eating Europeans and starvation.

After the fall of the Byzantine capital of Constantinople in 1453, the victorious Turks began disrupting the overland trade routes east from the Mediterranean. This caused pepper to be in short supply and prices to climb significantly. As a result of this "economic jolt," European explorers (and entrepreneurs) —looking for a second right answer—sailed west and south in search of alternative passages to the Orient. As historian Henry Hobson expressed it, "The Americas were discovered as a by-product in the search for pepper."

Another example of a disruption causing people to look for other right answers: after the Great Fire of Rome razed most of the city in AD 64 (during Nero's reign), Roman officials realized they needed to rethink their basic construction methods to prevent future conflagrations. The result was a radically upgraded building code in which the use of wood in beams was discouraged. This change allowed the widespread use of a fairly new building material: pozzolana-enriched concrete. This flexible material freed Roman architects from constraints such as right angles and allowed them to develop new shapes, such as the dome and the vault. The catastrophe of the fire served as a catalyst for architectural change.

Summary: The Wise Fool believes that there is always more than one right answer for any given issue or situation, and it's our job — when we're thinking like Wise Fools — to seek out these alternatives. We are invited to ask ourselves, "What's the second right answer in this situation? What's an alternative? What's just below the surface? If our current routine were disrupted, what would our third right answer be?"

Keep Playing with It

"I tell you, we are on earth to play around, and don't let anybody tell you different."

— Kurt Vonnegut, American Novelist

Let's take a look at seven examples of "wordplay," one each, respectively, from a novelist, an advertising copywriter, a scribe, a librarian, a priest, a codemaker, and a physicist. All highlight different aspects of play.

Wordplay #1: Irish writer James Joyce once mused:

Gee each owe tea eye "smells" fish.

What he was saying was that the letters "G," "H," "O," "T," and "I" *spell* the word "fish." How is this so? If you pronounce "GH" as it is in "rough," "O" as it is in "women," and "TI" as in "motion," it follows that "GHOTI" must be pronounced "fish." Is this just a goofy bit of frivolity? Perhaps. But the kind of playful thinking underlying it is the same kind that creates breakthroughs in subatomic particle theory, DNA research, and fun-to-use toys.

Wise Fools believe that play is an important lubricant of the creative process. When they're stuck on a problem, nothing pleases them more than an opportunity to play with it. For example, I have asked many people (actually, millions) when they get their ideas. The answers I've received can be broken down into two groups. The first is "necessity," and it is highlighted by responses such as: "When I'm faced with a problem"; "When things break, and I have to fix them"; and, "When the deadline is near — that's the ultimate inspiration." These replies bear out the old adage that "necessity is the mother of invention."

It's interesting that at least as many people report that they get their ideas in the opposite circumstances: "When I'm just playing around"; "Doing something else"; and, "When I'm not taking myself too seriously." This led me to conclude:

Necessity may be the mother of invention, but play is certainly the father.

The Wise Fool knows that you generate many of your new ideas when you're just messing around in your mental playground. You give yourself a license to try different approaches without fear of penalty. Your defenses are down, and you're likely to have little concern with the rules or being wrong. You try one thing, and then another — often not getting anywhere. You ask "what if" and "why not," put things in different contexts, and look at them backwards. And, eventually, you may come up with a worthwhile idea.

One person who would agree with this Wise Fool approach is cartoonist Bill Watterson, the creator of the much-beloved *Calvin and Hobbes*, a comic strip about a precocious kid (who doesn't have the experience to "know the things you shouldn't do") and his pal tiger. As Watterson put it in a 1990 commencement address at his alma mater, Kenyon College:

> Letting your mind play is the best way to solve problems. For me, it's been liberating to put myself in the mind of a fictitious six-year-old [Calvin] each day and rediscover my own curiosity. I've been amazed at how one idea leads to another if I allow myself to play. A playful mind is inquisitive, and learning is fun.

Wordplay #2: One of my favorite print ads was created in 1962 by Doyle Dane Bernbach copywriter Charles Piccirillo to promote National Library Week. The headline consisted of the alphabet in lowercase letters like so:

a b c d e f g h i j k l m n o p q r s t u v w x y z

Below it was this copy: "At your local public library they have these arranged in ways can make you cry, giggle, love, hate, wonder, ponder, and understand. It's astonishing to see what these 26 little marks can do. In Shakespeare's hand they became *Hamlet*. Mark Twain wound them into *Huckleberry Finn*. Gibbon pounded them into *The Decline and Fall of the Roman Empire*. John Milton shaped them into *Paradise Lost*." There are several messages here but to me the most important one is that creative ideas come from playing with and manipulating your resources — no matter how simple or limited they are.

Similarly, Wise Fools say a good way to play with a problem is to rearrange its elements. Like *Scrabble* players who move the letter tiles around in their racks hoping to catch sight of a playable word, Wise Fools love to rearrange the pieces of a situation until something promising turns up.

For example, in sports, a coach might juggle his lineup to improve team performance. In business, a manager might reorganize personnel to take advantage of changing market conditions. In warfare, a military commander might deploy troops in an unorthodox manner to outmaneuver an enemy. In music, a composer might reorchestrate a score's instrumentation to alter its feeling. In decorating, a designer might rearrange the contents of a room to give it warmth. And in film, a screenwriter might alter the typical story line to create a more compelling thriller. Indeed, as French director Jean-Luc Godard put it, "I like a film to have a beginning, a middle and an end, but not necessarily in that order."

Wordplay #3: Nearly three millennia ago, an 8th-century BC Greek scribe was trying to imagine ways to improve the reading process. Back then, the Greek alphabet (like the Phoenician one on which it was based) consisted only of consonants, no vowels. He realized that vowelless writing made reading a laboriously slow and inexact process. To understand a word, the reader had to guess the missing vowel sounds between consonants to grasp the meaning. For example, a modern English equivalent might be: does the two-consonant word "**FR**" stand for "**FAR**," "**FIR**," "**FUR**," "**FIRE**," or even "**AFRO**"? As with other cognitive activities, the letters' context and the reader's own personal experience would be the guides to interpretation.

Our innovative scribe looked at the Greek alphabet and playfully asked himself: "What if I looked at these symbols in a different way, and let some of the letters represent the vowel sounds we actually speak instead of only consonants?" The result was the creation of seven written vowels (*alpha, epsilon, eta, iota, omicron, upsilon,* and *omega*). By joining these new letters — vowels — with the existing consonants, he (and the other scribes of that era who contributed to and adopted this convention) created the first fully phonetic alphabet, that is, one capable of expressing all of the sounds in a language. This is an amazingly powerful invention! It enabled writers to translate spoken words exactly into written words, and readers to do the reverse. The result is greatly increased speed and comprehension. Thus, with the addition of vowels, these early Greeks gave new potency to writing and reading.

This story highlights another of the Wise Fool's favorite ways to play, namely, mixing and connecting things and ideas in new and different ways. Some examples: inventors combine components to craft new products: Johannes Gutenberg joined together the wine press and the coin punch to create movable type and the printing press. Entrepreneurs bring together resources from different arenas to build new businesses: the founders of Uber added a digital aggregator platform to smart-mobile technology to sync passengers and drivers in a real-time marketplace, thereby transforming the on-demand transportation industry. Metallurgists mix together different materials to create new ones: ancient bladesmiths alloyed soft copper with even softer tin to produce hard bronze.

Scientists marry diverse concepts to give birth to new models of explanation: naturalist Charles Darwin merged the idea of random genetic mutations with natural selection to arrive at his theory of evolution. Engineers integrate existing technologies to create new ones: a team of American military personnel united satellites, atomic clocks, computational algorithms, and radio transmitters and receivers to create GPS (the Global Positioning System).

Wordplay #4: One day in the 4th century BC, a Greek librarian had the task of storing away a large number of manuscripts that had recently come into his possession. He asked himself "What simple ordering system can I devise for these works so that I — or anyone else — can easily retrieve them later?" After playing with the issue for a while, he thought of the Greek alphabet — but not as it was usually conceived. His contemporaries considered it to be a series of phonetic symbols (*alpha, beta, gamma, delta, epsilon, zeta*, etc.) that were used primarily to form words that conveyed meaning. The librarian decided to de-emphasize the alphabet's word-forming function. By doing so, he was able to focus on a less apparent feature: each letter's relationship to the others in the alphabet. He thought: "What if I place those manuscripts whose titles began with *delta* before those beginning with *epsilon* but after those beginning with *gamma*, and use the same logic throughout. I'll create a storage and retrieval system that's simple and efficient." By ignoring the alphabet's linguistic purpose, he discovered its "ordering" power!

We use this kind of thinking when we playfully imagine familiar objects in unfamiliar contexts, say, looking at a "ballpoint pen" and thinking "weapon," or looking at "dried leaves" in the forest and thinking "toilet paper," or looking at stainless steel "spoons" not as eating utensils but as shiny metallic objects that could be used as implements in a "mobile."

Here's another variation of this kind of thinking. Suppose you were asked to determine what the following five words had in common: **crabcake, coughing, popquiz, understudy,** and **calmness.** At first, you might try a conceptual approach, say, looking at their meanings and trying to glean some connections between them. But if you playfully allowed yourself to shift your emphasis to looking at the words as merely strings of letters, you'd soon see that each one has three consecutive letters of the alphabet in it.

Wordplay #5: One of the most unheralded communication developments of the past 1,500 years is the adoption of spaces between words. Notice the words you're currently reading. They are separated by spaces and easy to read. Prior to the 8th century AD, however, Latin was written in a run-on fashion, that is, there were no spaces between the words. For example:

**WHENTHEREARENOSPACESBE
TWEENWORDSREADINGTHISIS
MADESOMUCHMOREDIFFICULT**

This type of writing slows down our reading. In ancient times, though, Latin texts were almost always read out loud (known as "reading by ear"). Ancient readers, because they were sufficiently familiar with their own language, could easily identify words by sound instead of sight, and had little difficulty.

Such familiarity wasn't always the case in later times. Eighth-century AD Saxon and Gothic priests, living at the periphery of the former Roman Empire, had a much weaker grasp of Latin, and couldn't always determine where one word ended and the next one began when reading Mass. The priests solved this problem by inserting spaces between the words in the sacred texts to serve as recognition aids. Over time, the addition of these spaces created an unexpected benefit: faster reading! That's because if you can see the beginning and ending of a word, you will recognize it more quickly. Moreover, the brain can sight-read words in much less time than it takes to speak. By the 12th century, most of the literate world had adopted spaces, and sight-reading became widespread.

The Wise Fool's takeaway from this "wordplay"? Look for and use the space around your ideas to highlight them and allow them to breathe! Along these lines, the esteemed pianist Artur Schnabel explained the secret of his artistry by saying: "The notes I handle no better than many pianists. But the

pauses between the notes — ah, that is where the art resides."
The 13th-century Sufi poet Rumi had similar ideas: "Every
craftsman searches for what's not there to practice his craft."

Wordplay #6: In the late 1830s, Samuel Morse and his colleague Alfred Vail had developed the physical components of
the electromagnetic telegraph, an invention that would radically change how humans communicate. Now they needed
a language that incorporated the basic units of their device's
communication: a coded arrangement of short and long elec-
tric pulses — dots and dashes — to represent the individual letters in the alphabet.

To increase transmission speeds, they realized that they
should use a shorter combination of dots and dashes for the
letters used most often. But what were these letters? They
didn't know because prior to that time not much research had
gone into figuring out the statistical frequency of English language letter usage. What to do? Why not play with the problem, and go looking for ideas in an outside area! Morse sent
Vail to the local newspaper — specifically its typesetting shop
— to get a sense of how often the various letters were used. Vail
inspected the typecases and found that there were 12,000 E's,
9,000 T's, and only several hundred Z's. Morse and Vail reckoned these numbers reflected how often the different letters
were used in communication.

These "typecase insights" led them to revise the original version of their "Morse Code." For example, they had planned to
use "dash-dash-dot" (— — •) for T, but changed it to a simple
"dash" (—). Likewise, E was now assigned a single "dot" (•),
and Z the more lengthy "dash-dash-dot-dot" (— — • •). These

changes saved telegraph operators from making many billions of unnecessary keystrokes in the ensuing decades! According to science historian James Gleick, information theorists have since discovered that Morse Code is within 15% of the optimal arrangement for minimizing unneccessary keystrokes in English text.

This story highlights another of the Wise Fool's favorite ways of playing with a problem, namely exploring for ideas, solutions, and inspiration in outside areas and disciplines. For example, mathematician John von Neumann analyzed poker-table behavior to create his "game theory" model of economics. Database designer Erik Lumer created a more flexible customer-profiling system for the banking industry by studying how worker ants cluster their dead when cleaning their nests. And World War I military designers borrowed from the cubist art of Picasso and Braque to create more efficient camouflage patterns for their tanks and artillery pieces.

Wordplay #7: Murray Gell-Mann, the physicist who coined the term "quark" for a class of subatomic particles after a line in James Joyce's *Finnegan's Wake* ("Three quarks for Muster Mark!"), was asked to share his reasoning for the names of the various types of quarks — "flavor," "color," "charm," and "strange." He replied with a smile: "The terms are just for fun. There's no particular reason to use pompous names. One might as well be playful."

Gell-Mann's comments highlight an important idea about play: one of its most significant by-products is fun, something the Wise Fool believes to be a very powerful motivator. For example, Rosalind Franklin, the scientist whose crystallography research was instrumental to Watson and Crick's discovery of the double-helix structure of DNA, was asked what motivated her. She answered, "Because our work is so much fun!"*

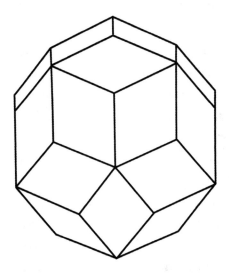

I love playing with geometrical solids — tossing one from hand to hand gets my creative juices flowing. I've been making my own polyhedra such as dodecahedrons (12-sided) and icosahedrons (20-sided) since I was a kid. Some years back, I was holding a 30-sided rhombic triacontahedron, and I thought: "How can I make this gorgeous object really fun to play with?" This led me to the idea of cutting it into 30 identical rhombic pyramids. I did this, and then inserted six rare earth magnets into each piece so that they became a kind of "design con-

---

* Physicist Richard Feynman had a similar philosophy: "Doing science is like sex: sometimes something important comes as the result of it, but that's not the reason we're doing it."

struction kit." Out of my desire for fun came the creation of the "Ball of Whacks" manipulative creativity toy. (And this has become one of my most popular products.)

Speaking of fun geometrical ideas, I recently gave myself the following problem as a way to discover new toy ideas: "Take a regular hexadecagon (a 16-sided polygon whose sides all have an equal length of *X*), and divide its internal space into 28 rhombi all of which have the same side length of *X*." After playing with it for a bit, this is one of the solutions I found:

What a gorgeous pattern! Maybe it'll lead to something new.

Summary: A "play with it" attitude allows you to manipulate the various pieces of the problem before you. The Wise Fool says: "How can you get into your mental playground? How can you rearrange its pieces? What previously unconnected ideas can you join together? In what outside areas can you go exploring? How can you make what you're doing more fun?"

Reverse Your Perspective

"You can't see the good ideas behind you by looking twice as hard at what's in front of you."
— Andrea Mercer, American Poet

The Wise Fool believes reversing your point of view can allow you to discover the things you typically overlook. Here are a few examples that illustrate this idea, including several of my longtime favorite stories.

In the mid-1950s, television quiz shows such as *The $64,000 Question, Tic-Tac-Dough,* and *Twenty-One* were huge ratings hits and revenue bonanzas for the networks. That is, until the "Charles Van Doren scandal" broke in 1958, and the public learned that the shows had been rigged: some contestants had been given the answers beforehand. These and other game shows were soon canceled.

A few years later, media executive (and popular talk show host) Merv Griffin was discussing with his wife, Julann, how much he missed the quiz shows. He knew, however, that their return was unlikely because their format had lost all credibility with the viewers. Julann playfully responded: "Why not give the contestants the answers to begin with and make them come up with the questions?" Why not, indeed! And then she said: "79 Wistful Vista." And he replied: "What is Fibber McGee and Molly's address?"—a reference to the old radio comedy program they'd both grown up listening to. It was quite the *reverse!* From this conversation sprang the basics for the long-time popular quiz show *Jeopardy!*

In the spring of 1954, a puzzling phenomenon took place in Seattle: drivers began noticing small pockmarks on their car windshields. As more of these tiny dents were discovered, a peculiar type of mass hysteria developed among the local population. Many theories arose to explain the cause of the pitting. One was that atomic tests by the Russians had contaminated the atmosphere, and this, combined with Seattle's rainy climate, had produced fallout that was returning to earth in a glass-etching dew. Another posited that Seattle's recently constructed roads were flinging acid drops against the windshields. Some theories even speculated that sand flea eggs and cosmic rays were the cause of the glass dents.

As people became more frantic, the U.S. federal government sent a team of scientists to probe the mystery. What they found was that there was *no increase* in windshield pitting at all. As reports of the windshield pits came to the attention of more people, they began to check their own cars. Most did this by looking through the glass from the windshield's *outside* instead of from the *inside*. This revealed the tiny dents that are almost invariably caused by normal, everyday driving wear. What had broken out was an outbreak not of windshield pitting, but of *reverse windshield viewing*. By reversing their viewpoint, people discovered something that had always been there but they had never noticed.

The Wise Fool says that a corollary to this Strategy is:

The second assault on the same problem should come from a totally different direction.

For example, educator Neil Postman relates the following story about how many centuries ago, an odd but deadly plague struck a small village in Lithuania. What was curious about this disease was its hold on its victim; when a person contracted it, he or she would go into a deep, almost deathlike coma. Most would die within a matter of hours, though on rare occasions a resilient soul would regain the full bloom of health. The problem was that because 17th-century medical technology was fairly primitive, the unafflicted had trouble telling whether a victim was dead or alive. But since most victims were dead, this was not a major issue.

Then one day it was discovered that someone had been buried alive. A distressed town council met to decide what they might do to prevent this from happening again. After a brief debate, the majority voted to put food and water in every casket. They would even put an air hole from the casket up to the earth's surface. This would be costly, but worth it if it would save lives. A minority group felt this proposal was too expensive, and they advocated a cheaper solution: why not implant a stake in every coffin lid directly over the victim's heart? When it was closed, all uncertainties about the victim's condition would vanish. What distinguished the two solutions were the questions used to find them. Whereas the first group asked, "What if we bury somebody *alive*?" the second asked, "How can we make sure everyone we bury is *dead*?"

Here's yet another example of using a reverse approach to solve a problem. A frozen-fish processor had trouble selling a new line of fish because consumers complained that the fish tasted "flat." The company tried everything to keep the fish fresh, including holding them in tanks until just before processing, but nothing worked. They had just about run out of ideas when an outsider happened by. He challenged the group's perception of the problem by offering this one simple suggestion: put a predator in there with them: that should keep them fresh. The idea worked like a charm. The fish kept moving to avoid being consumed, and as a result, they retained their vitality. There was some loss, but it was more than offset by a thriving market for their product. They discovered that a worthwhile solution was to be found not in pampering the fish, but rather just the opposite: scaring the living daylights out of them!

Reversing your point of view can also be a wonderful problem reframing technique—especially when you're repeatedly confronted with the same situation. Let's suppose that you're watching television in your den with some friends. A person walks in, and as he does, he trips over a chair and knocks it down. He picks up the chair and then excuses himself for the commotion he's caused. What's your impression of this guy? You probably think he's a klutz, right?

A few minutes later, another person walks into the room, and she too falls over the chair. Ten minutes after that, someone else comes into the room, and the whole scene is repeated again. What are your thoughts now? Well, if you have reversed your perception of the situation, you have likely come to the conclusion that the chair is in the wrong place and figured out that anybody else walking into the room will trip over it unless, of course, you move it.

The Wise Fool says approaching a situation in the opposite manner from your usual way can also help you find the things you typically don't notice. For example, when everyone else is gazing at the gorgeous sunset, why not turn around to see the blues and violets in the sky behind you? What stands out when you examine a tea cup? Its color? Its material? Its design? Reverse your focus and look at the empty space inside the cup. That's what creates its functional value!

Suppose you're a volleyball coach and you ask, "Rather than getting my team to play as a unit, what can I do to get them out of sync?" Your answer might be a list of things that would unsettle them. Then you could practice these things, because they'll likely have to deal with them in a game.*

Suppose you're in a grocery store buying produce. You see people around you jamming apples, grapes, and asparagus into plastic bags. You ask yourself: "What if I did this backwards? What if I put my hand in the bag, and then grabbed the produce and pulled the bag over it?"

Suppose you're in charge of improving customer service at your organization. Focusing on how to reduce complaints will lead to one set of ideas, while searching for ways to increase customer messages of praise to employees will lead to another

---

* Such a situation happened to champion swimmer Michael Phelps at the 2008 Olympics. After diving into the pool at the start of the 200 butterfly, his goggles began to fill with water. By the final turn, his goggles were totally filled and he was swimming "blind." Fortunately his coach, Bob Bowman, had made Phelps practice such an eventuality numerous times, and when it did occur on the world's biggest stage, Phelps calmly counted his strokes and finished with a victory in Olympic record time.

set. Similarly, by reversing their focus from *cure* to *prevention*, many doctors have moved the responsibility of health from the physician to the patient, forcing patients to become more knowledgeable about the factors that contribute to wellness.

The Wise Fool knows that doing the opposite of what's expected is also an effective strategy in competitive situations such as sports, business, romance, and warfare. In these endeavors, one side typically builds up expectations about what the other side might do. When the other side counters those expectations, it increases its chances of reaching its objective.

For example, psychiatrist Paul Watzlawick tells the following story in which doing the unexpected worked during wartime. In 1334, the Duchess of Tyrol laid siege to the castle of Hochosterwitz in Austria. She knew that the siege would take some months because the fortress was located on a cliff high above the valley floor. As time wore on, the defenders in the castle became desperate; their only remaining food was an ox and several bags of grain. The Duchess's situation, however, had also become severe: her troops were becoming unruly, and she had pressing matters elsewhere.

After pondering his worsening situation, the castle's commander hit upon a plan of action that must have seemed utter folly to his men. He slaughtered the last ox, stuffed it with grain, and threw the carcass over the cliff onto the meadow in front of the enemy camp. The Duchess interpreted this scornful message to mean that the castle had so much food they could afford to waste it. Because the castle's commander did the opposite of what the Duchess expected, he made her believe that her siege wasn't working. At this, the discouraged Duchess abandoned her siege and left.

Sun Tzu, the ancient Chinese strategist and author of *The Art of War*, would have applauded the commander's reverse tactic. A contrarian when circumstances dictated, Sun wrote:

All war is based on deception.
Appear weak when you are strong;
and strong when you are weak.

Life gives us many opportunities to use this counterintuitive approach to reach an objective. For example, have you ever: played hard-to-get to appear more attractive? Gotten away from a problem in order to solve it? Gone to the city to be alone? Embraced a fear to overcome it? Spoken very quietly to get people's attention? Adopted a child's outlook to gain wisdom? If so, you've used the Wise Fool's reverse technique.

*　　*　　*

During a lecture on major figures and events in the Second World War, my high school history teacher named: Dwight D. Eisenhower, George S. Patton, and Norman D. Beachhead. When I heard this, I broke out into laughter and couldn't stop (I had to serve an after-school detention for my outburst). I, of course, had misheard the name of the Allied D-Day invasion site and confused it with a person. That was my first formal introduction to "mondegreens."

A mondegreen occurs when you "mishear" an incorrect word, phrase, or slogan because of its "aural proximity" to the words actually being spoken and what is intended to be heard. Our language is filled with them — especially song lyrics. For example: "Lucy in disguise with diamonds," and "the girl with colitis goes by" (from the Beatles' *Lucy in the Sky with Diamonds*); "the ants are my friend" (from Bob Dylan's *Blowin' in the Wind*); and, most famously, "'Scuse me, while I kiss this guy" (from Jimi Hendrix's *Purple Haze*).

Mondegreens give us an insight into how our brains create meaning from the sounds we hear. If a misheard phrase makes sense, a person might keep using it, often with amusing results: imagine the girl who learned her *Hail Marys* in catechism as "Blessed art thou, a monk swimming," or the boy who learned that the technical term for weatherman is "meaty urologist."

Let's suppose that you're a puzzle creator and you're looking for ideas. You look at mondegreens, and think: "what if I intentionally created a *reverse* mondegreen, that is, an incorrect series of words, and then challenged the solver to figure out what was intended?" This is what the gifted crossword puzzle constructor Joel Fagliano did! On August 31, 2014, the *New York Times* published his puzzle (edited by Will Shortz) that was filled with mondegreens. It was called "Heard at the Movies," and it consisted of strings of random words, which, when spoken aloud, sounded like films that had won a "Best Picture" Oscar®. The clues to get the individual words were pretty easy, but they yielded these challenging reverse mondegreens:

WARDEN HAIRY PEEPHOLE
DWELL FIERCE SUSS LAVE
THUG ODD FODDER
HONDA WATT AFFRONT
HOW TOUGH HAVE RIGA

See if you can figure them out. This kind of wordplay isn't for everyone, but I thought it was a blast. Creating reverse mondegreens can be a fun activity, and you might try creating your own. Here are a few more: **GLOW BULL WORE MINK; MUG HUMP LEMONS TOO DASH HALF; CHERRY OTT SAPPHIRE; OOMPH LOUVERED A COOK USENET.***

Summary: The Wise Fool says reversing your perception of a problem can allow you to see the things you usually don't notice. This is a good way to free your thinking from deeply ingrained assumptions. The Wise Fool invites us to ask ourselves, "How can I reverse my perspective? How can I invert my objective or change my perception of it? What unexpected, counter-intuitive tactic might help me reach my goal?"

---

* Film titles: Ordinary People, Twelve Years A Slave, The Godfather, On the Waterfront, and Out of Africa. The other expressions: Global Warming, My compliments to the Chef, Chariots of Fire, and One Flew Over the Cuckoo's Nest.

Wise Fool Strategy #**7**

Fool Around with the Constraints

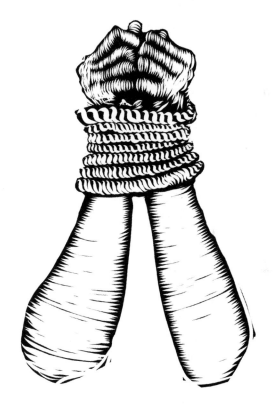

"Limits are an artist's best friend."

— Frank Lloyd Wright, American Architect

One of the Wise Fool's favorite ways to play with a problem is to look for solutions and possibilities outside the usual rules and guidelines. For example, in the 3rd century BC, the Greek city of Miletus experienced a sudden rash of copycat suicides by young women. The inspired solution of the city fathers to halt this? They decreed that any woman who committed suicide would first be carried naked through the marketplace before being buried. Did this violate their religious customs and norms of propriety? Absolutely, but the ancient historian Plutarch says that the city's unorthodox edict stopped the suicides cold.

Another example of this approach is the Macedonian general Alexander. In 333 BC, he and his army arrived in the Asia Minor town of Gordium to prepare for their upcoming military campaign against the Persian Empire. While there, Alexander heard about the legend surrounding the town's famous knot, the "Gordian Knot." Supposedly a prophecy stated that

whoever was able to untie this weirdly complicated assemblage of loops and twists was destined to become King of Asia.

Alexander was captivated by this story, and he asked to be taken to the knot so he could attempt to untie it. He studied it for a few moments, but after unsuccessful efforts to find the rope ends, he became stymied. He asked himself, "How can I undo the knot? I'll just play with the constraints and make up my own knot-untying rules." Alexander then pulled out his sword and sliced the knot in half. Asia was *fated* to him!

I have a Wise Fool friend I go to whenever I have a really tough problem to solve. After I explain it to him, invariably his first question is:

What rules can we break?

He knows that I have assimilated so many rules into my thinking that they've become blind assumptions. These make it more difficult for me to think of fresh ideas.

Think about it: almost every advance in agriculture, communications, design, medicine, art, sports, engineering, and science has occurred when someone played with (and challenged) the rules and then tried another approach.

By imagining herself to be a jazz instrumentalist rather than a vocalist, singer Billie Holiday tossed aside traditional stylings, and pioneered a "moving-around-the-beat" technique of lyric phrasing that influenced a generation of vocalists (including Frank Sinatra and Ray Charles). With his use of converging lines meeting at a single vanishing point, early Renaissance painter Giotto di Bondone ditched the Byzantine flat pictorial form to create space that displayed perspective.

With his equating mass and energy as different forms of the same phenomenon, Albert Einstein broke the rules of Newtonian physics.

By tossing aside traditional cosmological notions explaining how spiral galaxies rotate, physicist Vera Rubin gleaned the existence of "dark matter" and revolutionized astronomy's concept of the universe. With her sensuous love odes, the ancient Greek poet Sappho dispelled the idea that writing great lyric poetry was beyond the sphere of women's capabilities.

With his creation of reusable, low-cost booster rockets, entrepreneur Elon Musk challenged the rule that manned space travel was only possible within the realm of state-run agencies. By using female ground troops, snipers, and fighter pilots, the Soviet Red Army broke the age-old custom of "no women in combat," and increased their fighting potency against the German *Wehrmacht* by 40% in World War II.

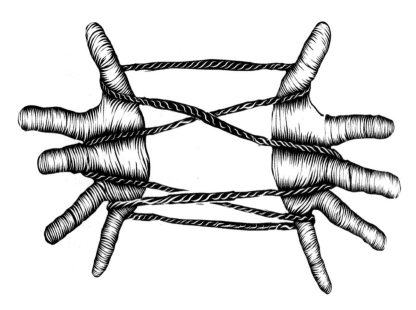

Wise Fools believe that giving ourselves a license to play with a problem allows us to try different approaches. Sometimes this means *removing a constraint* or two. But sometimes it means doing just the opposite: they know that an equally liberating form of play is to *add constraints to a problem*. Indeed, constraints can be a powerful stimulant to the creative process. If you've ever been asked to solve a difficult problem with a tight deadline and a small budget, you've probably found that you were much more resourceful than if you had been granted a ton of time and money. Constraints force us to think beyond conventional solutions and find answers we might not otherwise have found. For example, skyscrapers weren't developed by people with cheap, unlimited land, but rather by architects, builders, and engineers who wrestled with the problem, "How do we create abundant office space on small pieces of very expensive real estate?"

Photographer Ansel Adams discovered his expressive style as a result of an equipment shortage he faced while exploring Yosemite in 1927. As he was about to shoot Half Dome, Adams realized he had only one glass plate for his Korona camera. This "one shot is all you have" constraint led to his epiphany that what was most important to him was not creating a straightforward pictorial image, but rather conveying *the feelings the landscape aroused within him*, and then figuring out the mechanics for rendering these feelings. He called this breakthrough the birth of his "visualization technique." He accomplished his goal by using a sharp focus, heightened contrast, and a red filter to create his celebrated *Monolith: the Face of Half Dome*, the first of many extraordinarily evocative landscape images Adams made in his lifetime.

Cinematographer Roger Deakins (*The Big Lebowski, No Country for Old Men, 1917*) says a technique he uses to focus his thinking when filming outdoors is to "turn off the color of his camera's monitor and set it to black-and-white." This constraint allows him to concentrate more on the form and layout of the landscape, and to be less influenced by color when framing the scene's composition.

Similarly, Islamic artists were (and are) generally forbidden by the *Quran* to depict images of the human body and other recognizable life forms in their work. As a result, they channeled their passion for form into representing the geometrical patterns they found in the natural world. Their ingenuity is especially evident in the Alcázar and Alhambra palaces in Spain, where 14th-century Moorish designers crafted intricate symmetries in their wall and floor mosaics. (Interestingly, seven centuries later, physicists have determined that there are 32 different ways in which atoms and molecules in a crystal can be symmetrically arranged in a pattern and these are all represented in the Moorish mosaics!)

In a like vein, a poet may be more inspired by the challenge of writing a sonnet, which must follow a standard pattern of meter and rhyme, than by writing free verse. I have a friend who loves writing sonnets. He's invented a game in which he randomly selects six words, and then takes one minute to write a poem that highlights these words. He finds this exercise of adding constraints both stimulating and enjoyable.

Composer Stephen Sondheim has similar thoughts about the value of constraints: "If you ask me to write a song about the ocean, I'm stumped. But if you tell me to write a ballad about a woman in a red dress falling off her bar stool at three in the morning, I'm inspired." Indeed, it can be argued that the product of almost every activity—cooking, coding, and design to name a few—can be made more creative if you'd take some time to add a few constraints at the beginning of the project.

Adding time limits can also be a goad to people's creativity. I've discovered this in my seminars. When I assign specific, open-ended problems to groups, I've found that those groups that have less time to generate ideas (say, 15 minutes versus 25 minutes on the same problem) often have better and more creative solutions than the groups with more time. They tend to get right to the point, have less self-censorship, and are less concerned with proper protocol. (I like to work this way. If I have a project, I'll give myself tight mini-deadlines. This forces me to get rid of my excuses and dive right in to get some work done.)

And, finally: Mark Dunn's 2001 novel, *Ella Minnow Pea*, is an intriguing work that addresses how constraints affect human behavior. It's a story about the residents of the fictional island of Nollop, home to Nevin Nollop, supposedly the creator of the well-known pangram:

The quick brown fox
jumps over the lazy dog.

There's a statue dedicated to Nollop with the esteemed sentence listed on its base in a series of tiles. One day, the letter "Z" falls off the monument. The town's high council interprets this as an omen, and decrees that henceforth all words containing the letter "Z" will be banned in both spoken and written communication (for example, no words with "Z" in them, such as "zest," "dozen," "zipper," "zaftig," or "glitz"). The next letter to fall is "Q" and it is banned in all word usage as well.

As the letters continue to drop — and be outlawed — the townspeople become more upset, but they continue to comply with the council's oppressive edict. Their efforts to communicate within these constraints are both ingenious and sad — their culture is slowly eroding. With only five letters remaining (L - M - N - O - P), the heroine, Ella Minnow Pea, makes a deal with the high council: if she can figure out a pangrammatic sentence with just 32 letters (Nollop's pangram had 35), they will end the letter banishment. Just a few hours before the deadline, Ella remembers some storage instructions her father had given her:

Pack my box with five dozen liquor jugs.

Bingo! Her solution saves the day, and the high council restores all 26 letters to everyday usage!

Summary: The Wise Fool knows that a good problem-solving approach is to be flexible with the rules. Ask yourself: "What rules can I question? Which ones can I ignore?" Adding constraints to a problem can also stimulate our thinking. Ask: "What limits can I add to a current problem? What alternatives do they lead me to?"

Build on an Odd Idea

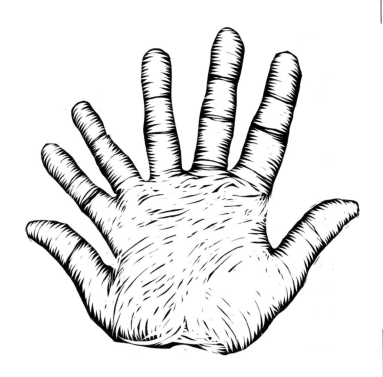

"If this unusual thing is true, what else is true?"
— Upright Citizens Brigade,
American Improv Group

The opening quote is the motto of the Upright Citizens Brigade, a popular improv group founded in 1990 by comedienne Amy Poehler, among others. It highlights the importance of having a positive, constructive attitude when dealing with unusual and anomalous ideas. Implicit throughout improv performers' engagement with one another is an outlook of:

"Yes, and . . ."

Such a perspective is vital because improv partners need to build on, rather than reject each other's ideas no matter how strange they are. For example, here are two improv performers working to create a scene:

> **Performer #1:** "Wow, I had a really busy afternoon at the bridge club."
>
> **Performer #2:** "I can see that—you've got some rivets caught in your pants cuff."
>
> **Performer #1:** [shakes out her pants legs] "Yeah, this bridge is going to span all the way across the Grand Canyon. You'll be able to walk from rim to rim in less than an hour."
>
> **Performer #2:** [begins running in place] "An hour? I gotta start training. I'm going to be the first one to cross it in less than 15 minutes."

What happened here? Performer #2 played off the ambiguity the word "bridge" to create a "construction worker" situation. If Performer #1 had responded by saying: "No, that's not right, I was talking about cards," she would have killed the scene. But instead, she built on her partner's comment to create the beginnings of a juicy improv bit.

Humor often uses this same principle. In his essay on the Comic, Sigmund Freud tells a story about a Marquis at the court of Louis XIV who entered his wife's boudoir only to find her in the arms of a Bishop. Seeing this, the Marquis walked over to the window and went through the motions of blessing the throngs of people in the street. "Why are you doing this?" asked his exasperated wife. "The Bishop is performing my function," answered the Marquis, "so I'm performing his."

What happened here? The Marquis, instead of pulling out his sword and slashing his wife and her consort for committing adultery, figured out a way to build on the situation. He thought to himself, "This is unusual; I know, *today must be role reversal day!*"

Like the improv performer and the humorist, when Wise Fools hear or think of an odd idea, their initial reaction is to say, "Yes, that's interesting . . . where does that lead my thinking?" Rather than dismissing it because of its strangeness, they will try to think of a context where the idea makes some sense and then build from there.

Wise Fools also love to propose odd and humorous hypothetical situations and then imagine their implications. In other words, they recommend asking "what if?" questions and then answering them. What if humans had seven fingers on each hand? You could name your fingers after the days of the week, and if someone did something you didn't like, you could flip them a "Wednesday." If you were clumsy, you could say, "Sorry, I'm all weekends." You might have several finger-opposing thumbs and likely have a better "grasp" on things. Would you be more sure-handed in sports? What kind of piano music would be written? Would there be more complex chords?

What if we could use AI machine learning tools to decode animal languages? We could feed several terabytes of dog barks into a program and develop a better idea of what they're saying to us. We could do the same with dolphin "whistles" and "clicks." Perhaps we could learn a few things about local ocean conditions from their intra-species gossip, and predict upcoming weather changes (this would be a boon for investors in commodity futures).

What if water decreased its volume when it reached its freezing point (like most other liquids) rather than expanded its volume? There would be less road and sidewalk damage in the winter when water fell into cracks on those surfaces. Also, ice would sink to the bottom of the oceans, resulting in a major diminishment of the polar ice caps. More easily navigable sea lanes might lead to a greater use of polar shipping routes (and shorter delivery times between Asia and Europe).

Many "what if" questions involve looking at familiar objects and ideas imagining what they would be like if they were put into different contexts. For example, imagine the first person to look at an "oyster" and think "food"; or the first one to look at "sheep intestines" and think "guitar strings"; or the first one to look at a "ship's sail" and think "windmill"; or the first one to look at "bacterial mold" and think "antibiotics"; or the first one to look at "packaged baking soda" and think "refrigerator deodorant."

Summary: The Wise Fool says that if something seems a bit unusual, take it as an opportunity to consider what possibilities it might create. What imaginative "what if" questions can you ask? Where do they lead your thinking?

Look for Ambiguity

**"The greater the ambiguity,
the greater the pleasure."**
— Milan Kundera, Czech Writer

What do the following (two jokes, a country music lyric, and an advertising slogan for a mattress company) have in common?

- "I was wondering why the ball was getting bigger, and then it hit me."

- "Think glass coffins will be successful? Remains to be seen."

- "If I said you had a beautiful body, would you hold it against me?"

- "For the rest of your life."

They all display ambiguity. Each provides us with words or phrases that can be interpreted in more than one way. In the first joke, "it hit me" refers to both the ball's collision and also the illuminative "aha moment." "Remains to be seen" in the second one refers to both uncertainty and a coffin feature. The Bellamy Brothers' country song lyric suggests both a proposition and a grievance. In the Sleepy Mattress tagline, "the rest of your life" promises both comfort and a durable quality product. When we discover the ambiguity in each of them, it's like getting a bonus "huzzah" after realizing the extra meaning.

The Wise Fool believes that we are "prisoners of familiarity" for much of our daily life. By that he means the more often we do something in a particular way, the more difficult it is for us to think about doing it in any other way. We get accustomed to thinking about things in only limited, specific contexts. To break out of this prison, the Wise Fool adopts an "ambiguous outlook," and takes delight in looking at things, words, and situations, and then wondering how else they can be interpreted. Indeed, the Wise Fool says ambiguity is our friend, and that wherever we can find it — most notably in the mundane bits of life — then we have discovered new possibilities in the world.

Here's a "fun" personal example. Not long ago, I underwent minor surgery that required anesthesia. It was my goal to remain in a relaxed, playful frame of mind (as much as possible) leading up to the operation. In the pre-op room, the head nurse asked me a series of questions, some of which dealt with my mental acuity (to establish a baseline to determine my cognitive state for comparison in the post-op room). She asked me to slowly spell out the word "world" (a standard question). I responded by saying:

W - H - I - R - L - E - D

She looked at me funny, and said, "Huh?" like I was missing something in the head. She asked me to do it again. I spelled it out the same way, and asked her to write the letters down as I said them. She then had a good laugh. First time in her many years anyone's done that to her!

How do we adopt an ambiguous outlook? It's easy: just ignore your initial response to the way you think about something, and then try to imagine other contexts where it might make sense. For example: how do you keep a fish from smelling? One solution is to cook it as soon as you catch it. Other possibilities: freeze it, wrap it in paper, leave it in the water, switch to chicken, keep a cat around, burn incense, and cut its nose off.

This last answer, "cut its nose off," plays off of a different meaning of the word "smell." This bit of cleverness is the result of adopting an ambiguous outlook and discovering that the problem could be interpreted in other ways.

Another example: look at the picture on page 103. What does it look like to you? If you look at it one way, it looks like a bird. If you look at it in another way, it could be a question mark. If you turn it upside down, it looks like a seal juggling a ball on its nose. What else?

Detective stories are a popular literary genre. Why? Probably because their authors use ambiguous clues, hints, subplots, and motives to build suspense and sustain uncertainty. The reader, in effect, becomes an active problem solver forming and then shedding one hypothesis after another as the story progresses.

Thinking ambiguously is also a useful strategy when you're dealing with riddles and puzzles. Solving them typically requires going beyond the apparent "first right answer" and imagining other contexts where the clue still makes sense. From my own experience, I can say that it's difficult to solve a medium-or-higher level crossword puzzle without having an appreciation for multiple possible meanings inherent in a word's clue. Here are a few crossword clues which exhibit this:

- "Man known for his double-take" can refer to a famous actor moving his head back-and-forth in disbelief, and also to . . . **NOAH**

- "Light-headed workers" can refer to employees at a Friday afternoon office party, and also to . . . **MINERS**

- "Place where you are charged the going rate" can refer to a fish market, and also to a . . . **PAY TOILET**

- "Remote spots" refer to faraway places like Tahiti and Timbuktu, and also to . . . **SOFAS**

- "Break one's word" can refer to backing out of a deal, and also to . . . **HYPHENATE**

- "Sleeping aid" can refer to a glass of warm milk, and also to a . . . **CLEAR CONSCIENCE**

- "Lemon grove" can refer to a citrus orchard, and also to a . . . **USED CAR LOT**

- "Veiled statement" can refer to a subtle threat made to an adversary, and also to . . . **I DO**

- "Party line" can refer to what a committed socialist adheres to, and also to . . . **SURPRISE**

- "It might turn into a different story" can refer to the court testimomy of a convicted felon, and also to a . . . **SPIRAL STAIRCASE**

To solve these sorts of problems, it's beneficial to have a Wise Fool whispering in your ear: "Keep imagining different contexts where this make sense."

History's most famous source of ambiguous statements was the Oracle at Delphi in ancient Greece. Supplicants consulted the Oracle because they wanted to look at their problems in a fresh way, and they believed that its prophecies would stimulate their imaginations. The savvy ones knew they needed to think ambiguously to discern alternative meanings in the prophecy's words. Those who didn't realize this fared less well. Here are two examples, one for each case.

In 546 BC, Croesus, the last ruler of the Lydian Empire (site of present-day Turkey), consulted the Oracle for ideas on how to deal with his enemy, the Persians. He received the following prophecy:

If you attack, a great empire will be destroyed.

Croesus took this as an encouraging sign, and led his army into battle against the Persian King Cyrus fully expecting to destroy the Persian Empire. Instead, he was soundly defeated, and it was *his empire* that was lost. Croesus' demise illustrates what can happen when we stop with the first right answer — especially if it's the one we had hoped to find. (Croesus should have had a Wise Fool to help him seek out other meanings!)

Another of the Oracle's better known prophecies came several generations later in the year 480 BC. The Persians (this time led by Cyrus's grandson, King Xerxes) had invaded Greece and conquered two-thirds of the country. In response, the Athenian city-fathers sent supplicants to Delphi to get a reading from the Oracle. They received this reading:

The wooden wall will save you and your children.

At first, they were unsure what it meant. Then someone suggested that they should build a wooden wall up on the Acropolis and take a defensive stand behind this barricade. But the city-fathers knew that the Oracle was intentionally ambiguous to force them to go beyond the first answer. They then tried to think of all of the contexts, both literal and metaphorical, in which the prophecy's words made sense.

After some deliberation, they came up with another idea. Could the "wooden wall" to which the oracle referred be the result of all of the Athenian wooden-hulled ships lined up next to one another? From a distance, the ships would indeed look like a wooden wall. The city-fathers decided that the battle should be a naval one rather than a land one. It was an auspicious decision as the Athenians went on to rout the Persians at the Battle of Salamis. The Oracle's ambiguity forced them to consult the deeper wisdom of their own intuition, and consider alternatives.

One of my favorite uses of ambiguity as a dramatic device is the classic *Twilight Zone* episode "To Serve Man" (teleplay by Rod Serling) in which an alien super-race, the Kanamits, comes to earth promising to give humans peace and prosperity. Initially, world leaders are wary of Kanamit motives. However, after code-breakers — with considerable difficulty — translate the title of a Kanamit guidebook as *To Serve Man*, they are receptive to see how the aliens might aid them.

The Kanamits' benevolent intentions are soon reflected by their actions: they give earthlings technology to create limitless energy and agricultural bounty, and also defensive force fields that prevent war.

With the world at peace, the Kanamits then invite the humans to visit their home planet, a place they describe as exotically beautiful. One of the code-breakers volunteers to participate in this "goodwill trip." As he is in the process of boarding the space ship, one of his colleagues runs up to the gangway. She has been able to translate several paragraphs of the guidebook's text and has made an astounding revelation. She exclaims: "Don't get on that ship! The rest of the book, *To Serve Man*, it's . . . it's a cookbook!" She's discovered — too late, as it turns out — that the guidebook is not an instruction book for providing good works to humanity, but rather a manual on how to properly cook humans for consumption.

Summary: The Wise Fool says a good way to be more creative is to seek out ambiguity in the world. You simply look at something and imagine other contexts in which it can be understood. Tip: If you are giving someone a problem that has the potential of being solved in a creative way, you might try — at least initially — posing it in an ambiguous fashion so as not to restrict the solver's imagination.

Wise Fool Strategy #**10**

See the Obvious

"You wander from room to room searching for the diamond necklace that is already around your neck."

— Jalai ad-Din Rumi, Persian Poet and Mystic

A young army cadet was being grilled at an officer candidate screening. "Well," said a ribbon-bedecked general, "what must an officer be before he can have a funeral with full military honors?" The cadet pondered this question for several moments, and then replied, "Dead."

In a 2005 commencement address at Kenyon, *Infinite Jest* novelist David Foster Wallace shared a parable about two young fish swimming along who encounter an older fish going the other way. The older fish nods to them and says: "Morning boys, how's the water?" The young fish swim on for a while, and then one of them says to the other, "What the hell is water?" Wallace made the point that a real education isn't so much about gaining knowledge, but rather about gaining an *awareness* of what is real and essential—and these things are often hidden in plain sight all around us. Wallace said that we need to keep reminding ourselves over and over: "This is water, this is water."

Many Wise Fools would agree: they believe that sometimes the most helpful ideas are right in front of us—hidden in plain sight—but we fail to see them. They recommend that a useful problem-solving approach is to identify our obvious resources, but they realize that this can be challenging.

For example, if you study the evolution of the bicycle during the 1860s and 1870s, you'll notice that both wheels start out at about the same size. Over time, however, the front wheel got larger, and the rear wheel became smaller. The reason was that the pedals were attached directly to the front wheel. Since there was no drivetrain on the bicycle, the only way to make the bike go faster was to enlarge the front wheel. The culmination of this trend was the "penny-farthing" model with a front wheel almost five feet in diameter (about 1.5 meters). Even though these bicycles provided a smoother ride than smaller wheeled bikes, they were also considerably more dangerous; "headers" (going headfirst over the handlebars) were a common peril for cyclists of that era.

The curious thing is that the solution for a better and safer bicycle was right in front of the bicycle designers. The bicycles themselves were manufactured using drivetrain technology! Finally, someone made the obvious connection, and asked, "Why not use a drivetrain to power the rear wheel?" Within a few years this safer model completely supplanted the penny-farthing. Remember: Nothing evades our attention quite so persistently as that which we take for granted. As the noted artificial intelligence scientist Philip Dhingra put it,

Only the most foolish of mice would hide in a cat's ear, but only the wisest of cats would think to look there.

A good (and perhaps obvious) strategy to find obvious information is to step away from a problem or a situation and ask ourselves, "What are the most obvious things I can say about this? What obvious resources are right in front of me? What stupid questions can I ask to help me cut through the details and see the basics?"

Another technique is to explain your problem or situation to someone who knows absolutely nothing about it. This should help bring the obvious aspects to the foreground. For those of you who are bashful or easily embarrassed, try explaining your problem to an imaginary friend. (For good measure, try explaining it to a stone age dweller who knows nothing of the things we take for granted: plumbing, antibiotics, instant communications, long human lifespans, etc.).

There's one other important thing to remember when seeking the obvious, and it is highlighted in the following story. It seems that Sherlock Holmes and Dr. Watson went on a camping trip. They pitched their tent under the stars and then went to sleep. In the middle of the night Holmes awakened and exclaimed, "Watson, look up and tell me what you deduce." Watson opened his eyes, and said, "I see billions and billions of stars. It's likely that some of these stars have planetary systems. Furthermore, I deduce that there is probably oxygen on some of these planets, and it's possible that life has developed on a few of them. Do you see that?" Holmes replied, "No, you idiot. Somebody stole our tent!" The point of this joke is that sometimes the most important obvious things aren't the ones right in front of us but rather the ones that *aren't*. If we're going to be resourceful, we should also take note of what's obviously *not present* (or *not happening*) as well.*

This point is also made in the Sherlock Holmes short story, "Silver Blaze," about the disappearance of a champion race horse. During the investigation, a detective asked Holmes: "Is there any point to which you would wish to draw my attention?" Holmes replied, "To the curious incident of the dog in the nighttime." "The dog did nothing in the nighttime," the detective responded. "That was the curious incident," re-

---

* Here's a charming example of dealing with what is not present. Topologists — mathematicians who study the properties of space and spatial configurations — enjoy exploring knots. To enhance their understanding, they also study the spaces the knots *don't occupy*. They call these spaces "not knots."

marked Sherlock Holmes. For our fictional sleuth, at least, sometimes the most important things are those that don't happen. In this case a non-barking dog provided a clue that the thief was probably someone the dog knew, and that fact considerably narrowed the list of possible culprits.

An oft-cited example of someone noticing what was not happening is the mid-20th-century Hungarian émigré mathematician Abraham Wald. Here's the situation where Wald applied this Wise Fool Strategy. During World War II, the Royal Air Force (UK) was dealing with significant losses of its bombers due to German anti-aircraft fire. A task force was set up to explore the possibility of adding armor to their planes. The central question was where on the planes to put it. To answer this the examiners studied the positions of bullet holes on the aircraft that had returned from their bombing runs. They discovered the following pattern: most of the bullet holes were on the fuselage and on the wing sections adjacent to the fuselage. They found many fewer holes on and around the planes' engines. A first pass suggestion was that more armor should be placed where the pattern of bullet holes was the densest — along the fuselage and adjacent wing sections.

Wald was a statistician on one of the teams analyzing the bullet hole data. Allowing himself to think like a Wise Fool, he wondered: "What obvious things should we be seeing here but aren't? Shouldn't we consider the idea that the anti-aircraft fire is hitting all parts of the plane equally, and not just the places where the examiners were finding bullet holes on the returning planes?" He further mused: "Why aren't we seeing planes with lots of bullet holes in the engine area? Probably because the planes hit there never made it back, that is, they were shot down. That's probably the weakest area." Wald's group recommended that if there were any reinforcement work to be done, it should be centered around the engines, and not in the places where the planes had already demonstrated an ability to survive gunfire, that is, the fuselage and nearby wing sections.

Political writer George Orwell noted: "To see what is right in front of one's nose is a constant struggle."* I think that he would have smiled and approved of this verse by his contemporary, the English poet James Reeves:

> The King sent for his wise men all
> To find a rhyme for W.
> When they had thought for a good long time,
> But could not think of a single rhyme,
> "I'm sorry," said he, "to trouble you."

Summary: The Wise Fool says, "See the obvious." Ask yourself, "What am I overlooking in this situation? If I step away from it, what obvious things can I say about it?" The Wise Fool also encourages us to flip our perspectives and ask: "As I look at my concept, what obvious things should be happening, but *aren't*? Why aren't they? What's not there but *should be*?"

---

* Here's one where I missed the obvious. I have a swim friend who recently turned 47. To celebrate his birthday workout, I created a quiz highlighting the number "47" with questions for him and his lanemates: Element #47 on the Periodic Table (Silver); "Best Picture" winner at the 47th Academy Awards (*The Godfather II*); 47th state to enter the Union (New Mexico); First person under 47 seconds in the 100 meter freestyle (César Cielo); Winner of Super Bowl XLVII (Baltimore Ravens); 47th prime number (211). I forgot until later this one (which should have been obvious to me): His favorite lanemate born on the 47th day of the year (me, on February 16th). Ha-ha!

Use Your Forgettery

"My 'forgettery' has been just as important to my success as my memory."
— Henry Miller, American Novelist

The Wise Fool believes knowledge is a wonderful thing, but that forgetting what you know — at the appropriate time — can be an important technique for gaining a fresh perspective. This is illustrated in the following story.

A teacher invited a student to his house for tea. They talked for a while, and then it was teatime. The teacher poured some tea into the student's cup. Even after the cup was full, he continued to pour, and soon tea flowed onto the floor. The student exclaimed, "Stop pouring; the tea isn't going into the cup." The teacher replied, "The same is true with you. If you are to receive any new ideas, you must first empty out your mental cup." Moral: Without the ability to forget, our minds remain cluttered up with ready-made assumptions — thus preventing us from asking the questions that might lead to new ideas.

One of my favorite workshop exercises involves making paper airplanes. I assign the participants to different teams and give each team 50 sheets of colored paper. Then I draw a line at the back of the room. Each team has five minutes to see

how many airplanes it can make that fly past the line. The one with the most is the winner. The most common approach is to fold the sheets into conventional paper airplane shapes. But the winning design is usually a sheet of paper that has been crumpled into a ball. These crumpled balls of paper invariably "fly" past the line — the only criterion that has to be satisfied in the exercise. When the losing teams see this, they immediately grasp that what had most hobbled their thinking were their assumptions about what a paper airplane is supposed to look like. The winning teams also held these same assumptions initially, but then conveniently forgot them.*

Similarly, folklore has it that the explorer Christopher Columbus challenged some Spanish courtiers to stand an egg on its end. They tried but weren't able to keep the egg from top-

---

* This exercise has a real-life parallel. In 1959, British industrialist Henry Kremer created a £50,000 prize to the builder of a human-powered aircraft that could fly 10 feet above the ground over a one-mile-long figure-eight-shaped course. For the next 18 years, scores of talented British teams built airplanes that fell short of the goal. In 1977, a team led by American engineer Paul MacCready won the Kremer Prize. The winning entry, the *Gossamer Condor*, was not much to look at: its unorthodox design — inspired by the sport of hang gliding — was essentially a huge wing. To paraphrase the observations MacCready shared with journalist Paul Ciotti: "The British teams' insistence that a man-powered plane should look like a plane doomed their efforts from the start. They seemed unable to make the conceptual leap that the goal wasn't to build an elegant human-powered plane with which they could win the prize, but to win the prize with whatever worked no matter what it looked like. We won because we didn't have the mental blinders that would cause us to dismiss out of hand the simple design that eventually won."

pling over. Columbus then hard-boiled one and squashed one end of it to create a flat base. "That's not fair," they protested. "Don't be silly," Columbus replied, "you just assumed way more than necessary."

One method for getting people to drop assumpions is to pose problems to them in an indirect way. This is a technique that the noted architect Arthur Erickson used to stimulate the imaginations of his colleagues and students. Here is an example of one of his exercises:

> Take a blank piece of paper and sketch a picture of yourself in a position of movement. After you've done this, provide a device (made out of plastic, wood, paper, or metal) to support that position.

At the end of the exercise, Erickson points out to his participants that they have been designing furniture. As he put it: "If I had said to the students, 'Look, we're going to design chairs or beds,' they would've explored the design on the basis of previous memories of chairs and beds. But by approaching the model from the opposite and essential direction, I was able to make them realize the vital aspects of furniture."

The idea of forgetting one's assumptions to find other answers is captured in this vivid epigram from the ancient Greek philosopher Heraclitus:

When there is no sun, we can see the evening stars.

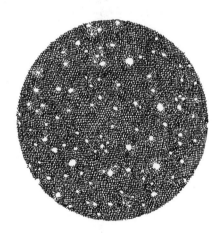

Here, the "sun" represents the dominant feature of a situation. For example: a noise that drowns out other sounds; a player who outshines his teammates; a strong spice that overwhelms the other flavors in a dish; an activity that leaves no time for anything else; and, the conventional way to solve a specific problem.

The "evening stars" represent the less obvious aspects of that situation. We don't see them because the "sun" is so bright. But when there is no "sun" — the dominant feature is removed — these "stars" become visible, and we become aware of other sounds, other players, other flavors, and other activities.

The Wise Fool would say this same "sun and stars" metaphor applies to how we think about problems. If we have a strong set of assumptions about a situation, we are less likely to think of alternatives. But when the dominant view is obscured or *temporarily forgotten*, these alternatives are more likely to become apparent. To say this in another way,

Discovery often means the uncovering of something that was always there but was obscured by something else.

For example, one day on his regular walk past the local blacksmith's workshop on his native island of Samos, the ancient philosopher Pythagoras temporarily ignored (or forgot) that the banging sounds produced by the smith's hammering of iron bars were "noise" — his typical reaction — and instead heard them as "information." This insight soon led to Pythagoras's discovery that musical pitch is a function of the length of the material being struck — and this became his first principle of mathematical physics.

Still another very easy, but quite effective, "forgetting" technique is to simply back off and get away from the problem altogether. As software designer Rick Tendy put it:

I never try to solve a problem by trying to solve it.

In other words, he recommends turning the problem over to the active powers of your unconscious mind. The Wise Fool understands that when you work on a problem or project, you plant a seed in your mind. When you back away from the problem, the seed continues to grow in your gray matter and to make new neural connections.

For example, take a minute and think of seven cities that begin with letter "C."

Now, that's pretty easy. You probably thought of seven cities such as Chicago, Caracas, Copenhagen, Calcutta, Columbus, Casablanca, and Cape Town. But now that the problem has been planted in your mind, chances are that when you wake up tomorrow, you'll think of seven more (Calgary, Cairo, Cincinnati, Coeur d'Alene, Canberra, Cologne, and Chennai), and continue to think of even more after that (Cleveland, Cusco, Chongqing, Charlotte, Calais, Córdoba, and Chattanooga).

Sometimes "forgetting" to do the next step in a process can be a good way to obtain some useful information. One of my very favorite stories to illustrate this point comes from designer Christopher Williams. An architect built a cluster of large office buildings that were set in a central green. When construction was completed, the landscape foreman asked him where he wanted the sidewalks between the buildings. "Just wait," was the architect's reply, "for now, plant the grass solidly between the buildings." This was done, and by late summer the new lawn was laced with pathways of bare dirt and trodden grass, connecting building to building.

As Williams puts it, "The paths followed the most efficient line between the points of connection, turned in easy curves rather than right angles, and were sized according to traffic flow. In the fall, the architect simply had the pathways paved. Not only did the pathways have a design beauty, they responded directly to user needs."

And, finally, a good way to forget about your current concerns is to get out in nature and work with your hands. Here's a personal example. About a decade ago, a friend said to me:

> If you get a bit blue in November when the earth is locking down for the winter, and you want to get your mind off things, try planting bulbs. You'll forget what's bothering you, and imagine new life in the coming spring.

I took her advice, and every year since then I've planted several hundred daffodil bulbs. Around my birthday in February, my hillside is a blaze of yellow.

Summary: The Wise Fool believes that forgetting what you know can be a useful means to gain insight into a problem. One way to do this is to ignore the initial right answers that come to mind when you're faced with problems you have seen before. Another is to approach a problem in an indirect way. This can allow you to see the things you usually overlook. Still another forgetting technique is to get away from the problem altogether. When you return to it later, more than likely you'll have a fresh point of view. The Wise Fool asks: "What is the 'sun' of your current situation? What new 'stars' come into view when you ignore it? Is your ego the 'sun' that outshines alternatives?"

Drop What's Obsolete

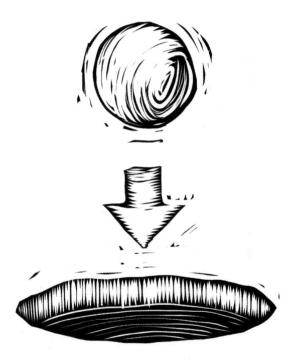

"Every 'right' idea eventually becomes the 'wrong' one."

— Peter Drucker, Austrian/American Writer

The Wise Fool believes that every strategy you employ that *leads to success* can over time become counterproductive and possibly *lead to failure*. For example, what a coach says to his players to motivate them in the preseason could backfire if said four months later when preparing the team for the playoffs. What produces results when a company is in start-up mode can be destructive when that company is expanding into mature markets. The sparkling characteristics that a child actor brings to a part when she is seven can work against her when she grows up and auditions for adult roles.

The Wise Fool urges us to continually update our assumptions and to make sure the strategies we use are suited to the problems and opportunities before us. This, however, is easier said than done. That's because there is a tendency for ideas, rules, and beliefs to remain in existence even though the original reasons for their generation have gone away. Thus, they can be very difficult to eliminate. Here are some examples.

There is an adage that the Prussian King Frederick the Great (1712–1786) lost the Battle of Jena, which was fought in 1806. The implication? For 20 years after his death, the army perpetuated his successful organization instead of adapting to meet the changes in the art of war. If his generals had questioned Frederick's sacrosanct military principles, they might have fared better against Napoleon.

Similarly, I once read about a group of Russian immigrants in Los Angeles who had the tradition of observing New Year's Eve on the afternoon of December 30th. A newspaper reporter asked them, "Why are you celebrating the arrival of the New Year 36 hours before everyone else?" One of them, a man in his 70s replied: "When we were growing up in the Soviet

Union many years ago, we were very poor, and we found that it was a lot cheaper to get a band on the afternoon of the thirtieth. That's how our tradition began." The curious thing is these people have prospered in America and could have easily afforded lavish entertainment on New Year's Eve, and yet they continued to celebrate it on the previous afternoon for a reason that no longer exists.*

Another example of this phenomenon is the "Pike Syndrome," so named after experiments performed to test the adaptive behavior of the pike. The pike—a long, lean fish with sharp teeth—is a ferocious predator whose main prey are smaller fish. The experiment was conducted in the following manner: a clear bell jar filled with water and minnows was placed in a large aquarium containing a pike. As would be expected, the pike lunged at the minnows. But each time it did this, it would painfully bang its nose and face. After many attempts, the pike finally ceased his attacks and ignored the minnows.

Now, here's the interesting part: the experimenters then removed the bell jar so that the minnows could swim freely—even right in front of the pike—but now the pike would not attack them. It had associated "pain" with the minnows and was unable to adapt to the new reality of an easily accessible, "pain-free meal." Like Frederick's generals and the early New Year's Eve celebrants, the pike was not able to understand that what he had learned no longer made sense because conditions had changed.

---

* Just about every organization I've ever worked with (including my own) has a bit of this mentality of "celebrating New Year's early" for some obsolete reason.

Whenever we settle into comfortable habits and routines, our thinking can become stagnant and inflexible. To get things stirred up cognitively, we need challenges such as solving problems, pursuing opportunities, having something at risk, dealing with novelty, and having our assumptions questioned.

One of the Wise Fool's favorite ways to stir things up is to "ask why" things are done the way they are — even in situations where it might be considered awkward. Asking "why" can help you (and others) examine their primary motivations for their policies and actions. It can also lead to eliminating obsolete ideas. This is how the American physicist Thomas Hirschfield put it:

If you don't ask "why this?" often enough, someone will ask "why you?"

Many people take pride in what they know. Wise Fools have the opposite philosophy: they believe *their ignorance is a valuable resource*. Indeed, one of their greatest powers is asking: "I don't understand why this is done in this particular way — can you explain it to me?" When we ask "why," we flourish. But when our curiosity wanes, our ability to detect problems and sniff out potential opportunities decreases. Why do some people stop asking "why," or at least do so less frequently? There are three main reasons.

First, during the course of living our lives, we simply get used to seeing things as they are. When you take things for granted, you're not going to notice much about them — let alone question them.

Second, we get intimidated by other people's opinions of

us. If you ask "why" too often, you run the risk of appearing ill-informed, or — worse — being labeled an obnoxious "pain-in-the-neck."

A third cause of diminished curiosity is complacency. When we're successful at performing a particular task, some of us have a tendency to think, "everything is fine," and stop looking for improvements. Obviously, this is a dangerous attitude in a changing world. As an antidote to such beliefs, the Wise Fool encourages us to ratchet up our dissatisfaction and focus in on those things that irritate and bug us. For example, I have an inventor friend who spends most of his waking hours tinkering with his work. I asked him why he did this. He replied:

**Because I'm dissatisfied with every-
thing as it exists in its present form.**

As a result, he has been able to channel this motivation into creating many interesting things. Some may say his method is extreme, but the Wise Fool would argue that a little dissatisfaction can be a beneficial prod in the creative process because it forces us to ask "why?"

Summary: The Wise Fool encourages us to examine existing rules and programs, and ask, "Why did this rule come to be?" Then follow this question with, "Do these reasons still exist?" If the answer is "No," then eliminate the rule. Remember: Innovation means not only generating new ideas but escaping from obsolete ones as well. As educator Rudolph Flesch put it,

Creative thinking may simply mean the realization that there's no particular virtue in doing things the way they've always been done.

The Wise Fool also asks: "What are you dissatisfied about? How can you turn *irritation* into *inspiration?*"

Wise Fool Strategy #**13**

Kiss a Favorite Idea Goodbye

"Kill your darlings."
— William Faulkner, American Novelist

One major reason why some ideas stay in existence past their "relevancy expiration date" is that people *fall in love* with them, and continue to use them even though better alternatives are available. The Wise Fool counsels us to avoid falling in love with ideas — especially the ones that have brought us success in the past. This can be difficult though. If you have had success with a particular approach, you can develop an emotional attachment to it — and that can make it challenging to eliminate.

Here's a personal example. Years ago, I made the mistake of falling in love with the *Palatino Semibold* font. Let me explain. When I started my company, I asked many people what special "business success" tips they could pass along to me. The best advice came from my printer, who said, "Don't fall in love with typefaces." He reasoned that if you fall in love with a particular font, you'll want to use it everywhere, even in jobs where it's inappropriate. I made the mistake of not listening to him. After awhile I fell in love with *Palatino Semibold* and used this typeface wherever I could — even in places where it clearly did not belong. Soon my design lost its freshness and looked hackneyed.

I think you can generalize this advice to "Don't fall in love with ideas." If you become infatuated with a particular approach, two negative things can happen: 1) You will want to use it everywhere — even where it is inappropriate; and, 2) You may not see the merits of alternative approaches and miss some opportunities. This is true whether the idea is a resource allocation policy, a school fund-raising strategy, or the criteria a couple uses to decide where to go on vacation.

The classic business example of falling in love with an idea is Henry Ford. A century ago, Ford had been successful making cars available in one color ("Any color you want, as long as it's black"). He believed that he had a formula that worked, and he did not want to change it. This prevented him from seeing the rise of a post–World War I consumer class that desired a variety of colors and styles from which to choose. As a result, Ford lost significant market share to General Motors.

I've personally known several founders of successful high-tech companies who were forced out by their boards because they didn't want to change their way of doing business. Like Henry Ford, they got too attached to an idea. I'm sure you've observed similar examples in your own experience where a person or group kept doing something in the same way because they were *in love with it*.

To deal with the issue of "idea adoration," the renowned graphic designer Paul Rand developed the following technique. Whenever he was working on a design that did not feel "quite right" to him, Rand would remove his favorite part of the design. Sometimes that would improve the design; sometimes the design would fall apart. But Rand felt this strategy gave him an opportunity to consider alternatives.

The French paleographer and Nobel laureate novelist Roger Martin du Gard had a similar approach for seeking objectivity:

The first rule—the "rule of rules"—is the art of challenging what is appealing.

He knew that people—including himself—can all too easily be attracted to illusions, orthodoxies, and dogmas of various kinds.

In a like vein, the 9th-century Buddhist master Lin Chi told his students:

If you meet the Buddha on the road, kill him.

Lin was not encouraging them to literally commit murder; rather, he felt that their symbolically turning a teacher into a sacred fetish missed the essence of both the teacher and his teachings, namely "don't get attached to things."

Several times in my life, I have had the privilege of watching Tibetan Buddhist monks create colored sand mandalas. These "paintings" are created by monks who shave sticks of colored stone into tiny grains so that they form intricately designed geometrical patterns on an area about the size of a card table. It's an amazing sight to witness: usually there are teams of four monks working at a time, and they are deep in concentration.

The mandala typically takes three days or so to complete. When the monks are finished, they admire the beauty for a few moments, and then say a few prayers over it. The head monk then scrapes the colored sand art into a pile and transfers the pile into a silk bag. The bag is then emptied into a nearby stream or local water supply. This symbolizes the ephemeral nature of any creation.

Summary: The Wise Fool believes that ideas have a tendency to stay in place even though the original reasons for their generation have gone away. Seek out obsolete ideas and then eliminate them. Having an emotional attachment to a past success or beloved idea can prevent you from looking for alternatives. What beloved ideas can you let go of?

Revisit a Discarded Idea

"Everything old is new again."
— Peter Allen, Australian Singer-songwriter

Wise Fools are big believers in eliminating obsolete ideas and beliefs. But interestingly enough, they also believe that sometimes there is a place for applying once-abandoned ideas to current situations. In other words, *the right idea can become the wrong idea, but occasionally—and under certain circumstances—it can become the right idea once again.* I've named this the "Thuban Phenomenon" after Thuban, the former and future "North Star." Here's the background.

Our current North Star is Polaris—the star around which all the other stars appear to rotate. But Polaris's role as the night sky's center isn't permanent. This is because as the earth rotates on its axis, it also wobbles like a spinning top. Over a 26,000-year cycle, the earth's axis draws a ring through the northern sky, and any star along that ring gets a turn as the "North Star."

One of Polaris's predecessors as a "North Star" was Thuban, a star in the constellation Draco. From roughly 4000 BC until 1800 BC, Thuban was the "guiding light" the ancients used to find true north. And what a "stellar" run Thuban had! The Egyptians used Thuban to align the great Pyramids of Giza; neolithic British tribes used it to lay out Stonehenge; and early Babylonian astronomers used records from a Thuban-centered night sky to create their highly accurate calendar.

But nothing lasts forever. Due to the earth's wobble cycle, Thuban has drifted away from true North and will move nearly $47°$ away from it by the year AD 10,000. But here's the fascinating part: Thuban will once again work its way toward celestial north, and by AD 20,300, it will be the Earth's "North Star." I wonder what amazing things will be conceived when Thuban again returns as the center of the night sky.

The Wise Fool believes that Thuban's movement from central importance to obscurity and back is a useful metaphor that can be applied to some situations in our lives.

Here's how it works:

1. You have a "guiding star." It could be an idea, a belief, an interest, a strategy, or a philosophy that guides your thoughts and actions.

2. You change. Just as the earth has its own perturbations, the axis of your life also changes. You develop new interests, you change locations, and you meet new people — such that you find new "guiding lights." And your original "guiding star" drifts toward the periphery.

3. Things continue in a "cyclical sort of way." Just as a former "North Star" can regain its central role, a former "guiding star" can once again take on a dominant position in our thinking. When this happens, the idea has "done a Thuban."

We've all known individuals who have been moved by a particular belief (politics, religion, personal interest) when they were younger, who then abandoned that belief, and who then returned to that "guiding star" later in life.

Indeed, I think that when almost anything has had a "renaissance," it is because people have gone back to an earlier era to find previously successful ideas and then applied them. That was the case during the Italian and Northern European Renaissance in the 15th and 16th centuries. The motto for the humanists of that era — Nicholas of Cusa, Pico della Mirandola, Erasmus, Sebastian Brant, Thomas More, Philipp

Melanchthon, Michel de Montaigne, Giordano Bruno—was *Ad Fontes*, or a "return to the sources," which for them meant borrowing from classical Greek and Roman ideas from nearly 2,000 years earlier. Looking backward helped them achieve their goal of moving beyond a religious-oriented medieval worldview and toward a more human-centered one.

Here is a variation of this same principle. I have a friend who likes to get ideas by reading old popular science magazines from the 1920s and 1930s. As he puts it: "There were many good ideas proposed then that couldn't be implemented because the materials weren't available. And so many of these ideas were shoved into the background or abandoned. However, the materials to implement them are now available. So these magazines are a gold mine of engineering inspiration."

Summary: The Wise Fool says that sometimes ideas and strategies that were successful in another era, but which have since gone out of usage, can be relevant once again within a new context. Thus, it is useful to look to the past for inspiration and solutions. Look at a current project that you've been working on for a while. Identify several ideas from its early phases that were tossed aside. Do they have any applicability in the project's later phases? What ideas from your own personal history can you apply to a current project?

Find What's out of Whack

"The first thing I do in the morning is brush my teeth and sharpen my tongue."

— Dorothy Parker, American Critic

The Wise Fool's tongue is the embodiment of her clever-ness. When her wits are sharp, she is alert and able to make discerning, often pointed observations. Sometimes her quips are acerbic—all the better to cut through their objects' pomp and pretense. A famous example is this exchange between two 18th-century British gentlemen who clearly did not like one another (the former a statesman, and the latter a radical jour-nalist who loathed upper-class hypocrisy):

> **John Montague:** Sir, I do not know whether you
> will die on the gallows or of the pox.

> **John Wilkes:** That will depend, my lord, whether
> I embrace your principles or your mistress.

Sometimes the Wise Fool adopts the role of a comedian or satirist. When she does, she articulates the incongruities that are part of our daily lives. For example, comedienne Joan Rivers once quipped:

A man can sleep around. But if a woman makes nineteen or twenty mistakes, she's a tramp.

Our initial reaction is laughter. But she also brings to the sur-face a cultural double standard, and this makes us think—even for just a bit—about some of the contradictions inherent in our own belief systems.

Pointing out incongruities is one of the Wise Fool's favor-ite activities. She enjoys shedding light on things that aren't quite what they seem to be, or whose reality belies their im-age. Indeed, she believes it is her job to "find what's out of whack." To do so, she activates her "crap detector" and sniffs out those things that appear to be operating in a contradictory fashion. Here are a few situations whose incongruity would likely invite her ridicule or at least a gentle spoofing!

A favorite target is hypocrisy, specifically, the discrepancy between what a person *advocates* and how that person actually *conducts* himself. A celibacy-preaching spiritual leader who has numerous affairs would be a worthy recipient of a Wise Fool barbed comment.* So would a carbon-demonizing celebrity who burns large amounts of fossil fuel on private jet travel to promote his ideas.

The Wise Fool also considers it her job to call attention to things that promise one thing and deliver something else. An example would be an economic system that offers free goods to everyone while simultaneously removing people's motivation to work hard or take risks. She knows that such a system could possibly lead to scarcity, and considers lampooning it a public service. (Of course, other Wise Fools would likely venture contrary opinions, and a lively discussion would ensue!)

"Design arrogance" is high on her radar. It's often found in products that are touted as being easy to use, but which in reality frustrate users and make them feel stupid. (Supposedly these products are "created by really smart people.") A surprising number of consumer items including software exhibit this and should be mocked.

Sometimes, the Wise Fool's recognition of incongruity finds

---

* A fierce example of calling out hypocrisy is Jesus's denunciation of the Pharisees: "Woe to you, hypocrites! You are like whitewashed tombs which look beautiful on the outside, but on the inside are full of dead men's bones and filth." [*Matthew* 23:27]

an artistic expression that deals with larger themes. A few examples (perhaps you've read or seen most of them): Mark Twain's *Huckleberry Finn*, a pastoral portrait of the contradictions of slavery's place in an ostensibly charitable Christian society; Stanley Kubrick's *Doctor Strangelove*, a satiric exposé of the Cold War's absurd triggering mechanisms; Joseph Heller's *Catch-22*, a spoof of the weird logic employed by the military's bureaucracy; Voltaire's *Candide*, a caustic look at the Catholic Church's hypocrisy in 18th-century Europe; Dante's *Inferno*, a tour through the Circles of Hell complete with a roasting of the arrogant and the powerful; George Orwell's *1984*, a sarcastic dystopia about a Big Brother government gone too far; and finally, Aristophanes's *Lysistrata*, an anti-war comedy about women who engage in a unified sex strike to force their men to cease hostilities. All of these works make us stop and think, "This is crazy! Could it happen here?"

The Wise Fool believes that a major way a discipline can be thrown out of whack is when a hefty dose of politics is mixed in with it. This is especially true when that slant — no matter where it originates on the political spectrum — is allowed to overwhelm the conceptual integrity of the field that it has entered. This has happened in many areas: entertainment, education, and journalism to name a few. But when it occurs in an enterprise that is charged with feeding a nation, namely agriculture, the results can be tragic. The Wise Fool asks us to recall the cautionary tale of Lysenkoism, a state-approved form of biology.

In the early 1930s, Soviet agricultural output fell significantly due to the forced collectivation of farms and the extermination of kulak farmers. The resulting famine of 1932–

1933 led the Soviet government to search for new farming methods but with the provision that these needed to be consistent with Marxist-Leninist principles. Up stepped a young Ukranian agronomist named Trofim Lysenko who concocted his own homebrew version of biology based on a single small experiment he did attempting to make a strain of winter wheat that could bloom in the spring. He claimed positive results for his work but it was never replicated.

There were two main thrusts to Lysenko's biology. First, he believed Darwin's theory of evolution had some valid points, but overall that theory's ideas about species competing for resources were too similar to capitalism, and this made them unacceptable to anyone viewing nature through the lens of dialectical materialism. Second, even though the Mendelian genetic model had provided biologists with useful insights for understanding the mechanics of inheritance, Lysenko rejected it because it emphasized the random nature of genetic mutations as the driving force of change, and he felt that this was a reactionary position. Instead, Lysenko adopted the widely discarded (but Marxist-friendly) Lamarckian concept that acquired characteristics could be passed on to offspring. (An exaggerated example would be cutting off a dog's tail and expecting that it would give birth to tailless puppies.)

Because Lysenkoism promised abundant yields ("we'll have orchards in Siberia") and was consistent with party ideology, the Soviet government supported this biological vision. Even Joseph Stalin personally gave it his stamp of approval. For most of the 1930s and 1940s, Lysenko and his supporters campaigned against other biological viewpoints and labeled dissenters as "purveyors of darkness."

By 1948, Lysenkoism claimed total victory. At a meeting of the Lenin Society of Agricultural Scientists, the USSR dictated that it was the only official biology, adding "we do not recognize the chromosome theory of heredity." Those scientists who had publicly disagreed with Lysenko were forced to write letters of self-incrimination admitting their "wrongthink." The ensuing purge caused over 3,000 mainstream biologists to lose their jobs. Some of these were jailed, and a few were executed. Classical genetics textbooks were removed from libraries, research laboratories were shut down, and all stocks of *Drosophila* fruit flies were discarded. Soviet genetic research was essentially destroyed. This was a major defeat for empirical science.

Even though Soviet agricultural yield continued to decline, Lysenkoism—with its politically correct ideological underpinnings—still held sway throughout most of the 1950s, both in the Soviet Union and also in its Eastern Bloc satellite nations. Only in the early 1960s did its influence wane. Unfortunately, a whole generation of Soviet biologists had been lost. This included many who had tried "flexing their risk muscles" against the state's political intrusion, among them the noted geneticist Nikolai Vavilov (who died in a prison camp in 1943).

Summary: The Wise Fool asks: "What's out of whack in your current situation? What contradictions, incongruities, and hypocrisy do you see? Is there a dogma or political view that is dominating your thinking?"

Stop Fooling Yourself

"The first principle is that you must not fool yourself, and you are the easiest person to fool."
— Richard Feynman, American Physicist

The Wise Fool knows that deception is a fundamental part of life. This artfulness occurs at all levels—from gene to cell to individual to group. Viruses and bacteria practice it: for example, HIV changes coat proteins so often that the host has a difficult time mounting a defense against it. Plants, insects, and virtually all members of the animal kingdom also have ways of deceiving the other organisms in their surroundings. Many orchid species are pollinated by offering their pollinators *only the illusion* of something they desire but not its reality. Animals camouflage themselves for protection against predators: the skin of octopuses can change color in mere seconds.

On the human level, deception runs deep in our interactions with others. We see it in war: commanders feign weakness to lure an enemy into battle, or fake strength to prevent an enemy attack. In politics and courtship, politicians and lovers hide character flaws. In statecraft, governments mislead their citizens with flowery promises about programs that will contribute to the common good, but that in fact often benefit only an elite few. In riddles, puzzlers use equivocal and extraneous information to delude would-be solvers into making false assumptions. In sports, teams disguise plays to confuse their opponents. Poker players fool their opponents with misleading "tells."

Many of us receive our first exposure to deception in fairy tales, such as the bad wolf disguising himself as Granny in "Little Red Riding Hood," or the evil witch luring Hansel and Gretel into her house with false promises.

The lessons of many of the Brothers Grimm fairy tales are plain: the rewards go not so much to the virtuous or the deserving, but rather to those who recognize deceit and think

on their feet. The Wise Fool believes the lesson of "don't be fooled" is an important one for both young and old alike!

As much as our environment deceives us, however, the Wise Fool believes that the "champion fooler" in our daily experience is not the world itself, but *ourselves*. That's because self-deception plays an enormous role in how we navigate our way through life. Indeed, the Wise Fool believes that our judgment would be greatly improved if we were more honest with ourselves about our own cognitive limitations. Physicist Richard Feynman would agree. He uttered the words in the quote at the beginning of this section at his 1974 Cal Tech commencement address. There he encouraged his audience — primarily scientists and engineers — to entertain the possibility that they were more biased in their outlook than they had imagined, and to strive for greater objectivity in their work.

Feynman recognized this would be difficult, however, because most people have many unconscious assumptions — perceptual, cognitive, political, and cultural to name but a few — built into their thinking, and they are rarely aware of their presence. Feynman understood that it takes a significant effort to minimize these biases, and felt that those who think differently are fooling themselves.

How easily are we fooled? Just a few minutes paging through a book of optical illusions should dent your certainty that you can readily discern the "truth" of a situation. If you talk to professional illusionists — magicians — they would say that humans are "very easily fooled." Teller, the silent half of the Penn and Teller magic team, has said that cognitive scientists are neophytes when it comes to researching human perception — at least compared to magicians, who have been studying the subject for thousands of years. His conclusion is that we constantly deceive ourselves — especially in the credence we give to our perceptions. As Teller bluntly puts it:

Nothing fools us better than the lies we tell ourselves.

Perhaps the biggest lie we tell ourselves is our notion that the construction we make of the world in our heads is a fairly objective representation of reality. This is far from the truth. When we perceive something, we do not see it as it is. Cognitive scientists have shown that human perception is a complex process in which our brains create mental images of the external world based on our shaping, distorting, and censoring information obtained from the senses.

This leads to a big cognitive blind spot. Many of us see ourselves as free of perceptual constraints, social biases, and cultural influences — at least compared to other people. Because of this conceit, we fail to appreciate how significantly our decision-making and problem-solving skills are impacted. This is what Feynman warned us about.

This distortion in judgment is especially true in how we evaluate our own work and worth. People routinely self-inflate their own competency, and put themselves in the top half of distributions of positive traits and in the lower half of negative ones. Several amusing statistics from "self-deception expert" Robert Trivers: over 80% of U.S. high school students rank themselves in the top half of leadership abilities. Academics are worse: 94% rank themselves in the top half of their professions.

Such self-deception is at the forefront of Lawrence Kasdan's 1983 film, *The Big Chill*, about a group of college cohorts who reunite at the funeral of a friend 15 years after their graduation. In one scene, two characters (Michael, a journalist played by Jeff Goldblum, and Sam, a television action star played by Tom Berenger) are discussing how the mind lies to itself:

Michael: I'm just trying to get what I want — which is what everybody does.

Sam: Why is it that what you just said strikes me as a massive rationalization?

Michael: Don't knock rationalizations. I don't know anyone who could get through the day without a few juicy rationalizations. They're more important than sex.

Sam: Aw, come on. More important than sex?

Michael: Oh yeah? Ever gone a week without a rationalization?

Each of us has a veritable "cognitive stew" of influences affecting our judgment. If you look at the *Wikipedia* entry of "cognitive bias," you find that psychologists have identified over 150 different types that show how significantly we color our thinking and perception.* Here are just a few of them:

- People remember humorous items than more non-humorous ones (*Humor Effect*).

- People place greater value on something they have partially assembled (*IKEA Effect*).

- People underestimate the time to travel much-used routes and overestimate the duration to travel unfamiliar routes (*Time Travel Bias*).

Our judgment is obviously also guided by our culture. However, we have often inculcated our cultural assumptions so deeply into our thinking that we're not even aware how much they guide our behavior. One easy way to understand how our culture shapes our thinking is to leave it. For example, some years ago when I was living in Germany, I went to a New Year's Eve party in Hamburg. It was a pleasant evening with good food and good people. Around ten-thirty, someone brought

---

* Business management writer Tom Peters has an interesting take on this topic: "I have spent so much time studying cognitive biases that I almost believe that anything that 'makes sense' isn't true." Does *his* comment make *any sense*?

out a big bowl of popcorn. I thought, "This is great, I haven't had popcorn in over six months," and reached in and stuck a big handful in my mouth. Boy, was I surprised: somebody had put sugar on the popcorn. I, of course, was expecting salt. As I learned that evening, in parts of Northern Europe it's customary to put sugar on popcorn. But in my world, salt was popcorn's obvious (and unquestioned) flavor enhancer.

A more curious example of how different cultures map out the (usually subliminal) behavior patterns that their members follow is psychiatrist Paul Watzlawick's description of the clash that occurred when American soldiers dated English women during World War II. It seems that both the men and the women accused each other of being sexually aggressive. What caused this? Confused cues. Anthropologists say that every culture has a courtship procedure consisting of approximately 30 steps beginning with first eye contact on through to the consummation of the relationship. The interesting thing is that not every culture has these steps in the same place. In the North American pattern, kissing is about #5 — it's a friendly way of getting the relationship started. In pre–World War II England, however, kissing was about step #25 — it was considered a highly erotic activity.

Now imagine what would happen when an American GI and an English woman would get together. They would go out, have a date or two, and then the soldier would think, "I'll give her a kiss to get this relationship going." He kisses her and she is astounded. She thinks, "This guy is creepy and oversexed. Kissing isn't supposed to happen until later." Furthermore, she feels (consciously or unconsciously) like she's just been cheated out of 20 steps in the courtship process.

But now she must make a decision: either break off the relationship because it has moved too far too fast, or get ready for intercourse because it is only five steps away. From the man's point of view, the situation is equally confusing: she acts either like a woman in hysteria or a nymphomaniac. The moral of these stories: if life is a game, each culture makes different rules. Often we're quite unaware just how much our perception and behavior are guided by them.

Summary: The Wise Fool says to be on the lookout for deception. Is it possible that someone has disguised their intentions from you? The Wise Fool also says you are fooling yourself if you believe you have a truly objective view of the world. The reality is that you are more biased and influenced by unconscious assumptions than you would like to admit. The Wise Fool encourages us to ask ourselves: "How am I fooling myself? Is it possible I'm less competent in understanding this problem than I thought? What do I believe to be true that's really not? What have I misunderstood?"

The Wise Fool says that it's also good to remember Postman's Law (after educator Neil Postman):

**At any given time, the chief
source of the crap you have to
deal with is yourself.**

Wise Fool Strategy #**17**

Exercise
Humility

"I tell you Wellington is a bad general,
the English are bad soldiers; we will
settle this matter before lunchtime."

— Napoleon Bonaparte,
French General and Emperor

At breakfast on June 18, 1815, a few hours before the Battle of Waterloo, Napoleon Bonaparte smugly assured his generals with the just-cited comment. By sundown of that evening, he and his army had been routed from the battlefield, and he was days away from being shipped off to a tiny spit of land in the South Atlantic to spend his final years in exile.

The Wise Fool believes that self-confidence is essential to our success as creative human beings. That's because when we create new things, we expose ourselves to failure, frustration, ridicule, and rejection. Thus, it can take a strong sense of our own worth for us to persevere and make our ideas a reality.

There is, however, a fine line between a healthy sense of one's abilities and arrogance. If we are repeatedly successful, we are tempted to believe that we have found the formula for success and are no longer subject to human fallability. This is devastating to our judgment. As the Wise Fool has already noted, in a world that is continually changing, every right idea is eventually the wrong one. With an arrogant attitude, we cease paying attention to different points of view and information that contradicts our beliefs. We screen out the "boos" and amplify the "hurrahs." We believe that we're not subject to the same constraints as others.

Shortly before the Chernobyl (Ukraine) nuclear reactor melted down and exploded in 1986, its engineering team — comprised of respected experts—won a distinguished award for operations excellence. The team felt that the safety rules they were asked to follow were designed much too narrowly for such an experienced group, and so they disregarded them during their reactor experiments. The result was a catastrophe, with loss of human life and potential damage to future generations.

Think of all the businesses that were so sure of their products that they stopped listening to their customers and soon found themselves without any. Similarly, the history of warfare is filled with military leaders who became intoxicated with their successes and then overreached in subsequent campaigns: Alexander in Afghanistan, Napoleon in Russia, Hitler in Russia, the French in Indochina, the Americans in Vietnam, the Soviets in Afghanistan. Arrogance can infect entire cultures. The Chinese were confident of their superior ways shortly before they were conquered by the Mongols. The same could be said about the Aztecs and the Incas prior to the arrival of the Spanish. The ancient Greek word for arrogance is *hubris*, and it was seen as a precursor to one's downfall. Anyone proud enough to challenge the gods will be burned by the gods. As surely as night follows day, destruction follows arrogance. Indeed, the Wise Fool emphatically agrees with this 2,500-year-old sentiment from the ancient Greek philosopher Heraclitus:

There is a greater need to extinguish arrogance than a blazing fire.

Think back to what people believed 100 years ago — especially the things about which they felt great certainty. How much of what was accepted then is still thought to be credible today? How about ideas from as recently as thirty years ago? How well do they hold up?

For example, Florian von Donnersmarck's 2006 film, *The Lives of Others*, presents a graphic portrait of how the dreaded Stasi (East Germany's State Security Service) unscrupulously surveilled its own citizens in the 1980s — in the movie's case, a prominent playwright — by hiding microphones throughout their apartments, and then listening in for any incriminating conversations they might have with their associates. Now jump to the present. Imagine how amazed a Stasi officer from that era would be to discover that people today not only buy listening devices (Alexa, Siri, Nest, etc.) and willingly install them in their own homes so their activities can be monitored by distant computers, they also carry GPS locators in their pockets so they can be tracked wherever they go!

If history is any guide, it shows us that it is likely that a good portion of what we hold to be true today probably won't be regarded as so a century from now — at least not with the same conviction. For one thing, many of our tools for knowing will have changed significantly. This should give us pause for how much certainty we assign to what we assert to be true, and also another reason why it is good to have some humility in your Wise Fool outlook. Indeed, humility is an excellent problem-solving tool. Socrates, history's all-time great Wise Fool, used it as the starting point for his philosophical inquiry:

All I know is that I know nothing.

When we are humble about the limits of our knowledge (and are able to put aside strongly held beliefs), we are more open to other approaches. Pride, humility's opposite number, brings in many curses; chief among them is having to defend existing points of view. A humble mindset gives us the freedom to appreciate that there are good and great things beyond ourselves and to learn from them. The ancient Chinese educator Confucius reportedly expressed a similar sentiment:

Real knowlege is to know one's ignorance.

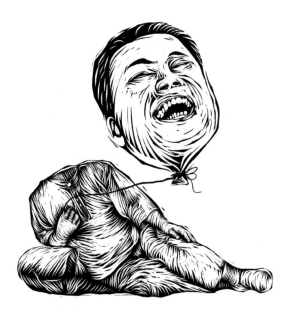

Investor and risk philosopher Nassim Nicholaus Taleb agrees that a grounding in humility is useful in exploring ideas and making decisions: "I start every meeting at my firm by convincing everyone that we are a bunch of idiots who know nothing and are mistake-prone, but happen to be endowed with the rare privilege of knowing it."*

---

* The 20th-century Jewish philosopher Martin Buber had a similar philosophy. Here's a paraphrase of Buber's discussion of an idea from the Rabbi Simcha Bunin: "You should have two pockets into which you can reach according to your needs. In your right one, keep a note with the words: **'For my sake the world was created.'** In your left, have one with: **'I am dust and ashes.'** Depending on your circumstances, both notes can help you. If you need a shot of confidence, consult your right pocket. But this should be balanced by occasionally looking into your left one to get a jolt of humility." Buber reckoned that this will protect us from overreaching.

One final thought about arrogance: if you consistently display a "high and mighty" attitude, the people who work with you will look for ways to take you down a peg or two. This is something the 18th-century soprano Adriana Ferrarese should have kept in mind. The central role of "Fiordiligi" in the 1790 opera *Così fan tutte* had been written for her by the librettist Lorenzo Da Ponte. She also happened to be Ponte's mistress. Being a prima donna can make one arrogant, but being the lover of the show's creator made her insufferable. The orchestrator of this opera, however, was none other than Wolfgang Amadeus Mozart, and he held little affection for Ferrarese. Mozart had worked with her on a previous opera, *The Marriage of Figaro*, and he had endured enough of her demands and antics. How would he respond? Through his music, naturally! It seems that Ferrarese had the odd tendency of bowing her head when she sang the low notes and raising it high when she sang the high ones. For fun, Mozart scored her signature aria, *Come scoglio* ("Like a Rock"), with many alternating high and low notes. He and the other cast members took pleasure in watching her bob her head up and down "like a chicken" while performing it.

Summary: The Wise Fool cautions us to examine how past successes have shaped our judgment — especially if these successes have spawned "I can't fail" beliefs. Arrogance leads us into thinking that whatever we do will give us the desired result. Ask yourself "How is my ego adversely affecting my judgment? Has success made me less receptive to alternative approaches?" Remember the Roman Stoic philosopher Seneca's method for grounding himself: "If I want to see a fool, I have only to look in the mirror."

Imagine the Unintended

"The only ironclad rule of human experience has been the law of unintended consequences."

— Ian Tattersal, British/American Paleoanthropologist

The Wise Fool understands that the fabric of our world is held together by forces that are complex, continually changing, and often beyond the limits of human discernment. Thus, implementing our ideas can sometimes have the unintended consequence of causing the opposite of what we want to occur. It's as though the cosmos enjoys a good laugh at our folly of thinking we can control the outcomes of events we set in motion.

This idea seems to be embedded deeply in the human psyche. For example, remember the classic story of King Midas? According to legend, Midas so loved gold that when the god Dionysus offered to grant his deepest wish, he asked that all he touched be turned into this precious metal. At first, Midas was delighted with his wealth-creating power, but when he discovered that his contact made food inedible and loved ones lifeless, he soon realized that getting what you want can have unintended — and undesirable — consequences. Here are some examples of this phenomenon.

In preparing for the Olympics, the coach of a leading crew team invited a meditation instructor to teach mindfulness techniques to his crew. He hoped that such training would enhance their rowing effectiveness and improve their sense of unity. As the crew learned more about meditation, they became more synchronized, their strokes got smoother, and there was less resistance. Just what the coach wanted! The irony is that their performance decreased and they went slower. It turned out that the crew was more interested in being in harmony than in winning. So the meditation teacher was dismissed.

Around the early 1900s, wolves threatened animals in and near Yellowstone National Park. To combat this dire economic threat, the federal government implemented an "antipredator" program that successfully eradicated the wolf population. In the ensuing years, however, the wolves' absence allowed elk to proliferate and devour the region's aspen saplings and other vegetation. This deprived beavers and birds of their native habitat and food. Without beaver-made ponds and seed dispersal by the birds, fewer succulents grew in the spring, which meant significantly less food for grizzly bears emerging from hibernation. In short, the elimination of the wolf caused many of the area's ecosystems to break down and seriously eroded the area's biological vibrancy and economic well-being.*

In 1906, after a series of negative newspaper stories detailing multiple predatory business practices by the Standard Oil Company and its leader John D. Rockefeller, public opinion turned solidly against the giant petroleum trust and the business tycoon. Responding to populist forces "calling for blood," President Theodore Roosevelt and several states attorneys general used the Sherman Antitrust Act to go after the huge oil monopoly. Their motives were to punish Rockefeller and Standard Oil for their alleged collusion dating back to the 1870s. In 1911, the United States Supreme Court ordered the oil giant to be broken up into 30 smaller companies. As things played out after the verdict, the breakup had a different impact from the one that the trustbusters may have hoped for. The pre-1900 Standard Oil had been primarily an

---

* In 1995, gray wolves were reintroduced into the region, causing an increase of new-growth vegetation among aspen and willow trees, an increase in the beaver population, and the subsequent improvement of marsh and pond habitats.

illuminant giant — its main business was providing fuel oil for kerosene lamps. By 1910, however, the petroleum industry was going through a major transition as oil companies began selling gasoline in growing quantities due to the boom in automobile ownership. The breakup allowed the newly established companies to jettison a number of longtime senior managers who had been slow to refocus on the new business opportunities. As a result, these smaller companies became nimbler, and even more aggressive than the pre-1900 Standard Oil Company had been. Indeed, many of these new companies became behemoths in their own right: Standard Oil of New Jersey became what was later to be known as Exxon; Standard Oil of New York became Mobil; Standard Oil of Indiana became Amoco; Standard Oil of California became Chevron, and so on. In addition, the 1911 breakup, rather than punishing Rockefeller, rewarded him: his net worth *doubled* during the next year alone, and grew significantly in the ensuing years.* Thus, the antitrust actions had the ironic consequence of both revitalizing the surviving companies and also enriching the world's wealthiest man.

During the the Soviet-Afghan war (1979–1988), the Soviets unleashed brutal attacks on the civilian population, believing that this would intimidate the Afghans into submission. Ironically, the attacks had an unexpected and opposite result. Because Afghan warriors traditionally stayed close to home to guard their families, the Soviets' driving Afghan women and

---

* According to historian Ron Chernow, these funds allowed the Rockefeller Foundation to pour vast sums into its main beneficiaries: medicine (research), and education, specifically to aid historically Black colleges and universities (HBCUs).

children into refugee camps liberated the Mujahideen from family responsibilities and turned them into a more formidable opponent. (American funding of the Afghan warriors came back to bite them as this resistance movement morphed into anti-Western Jihadist groups such as al-Qaeda, the Taliban, and ISIS in the 1990s, 2000s, 2010s, 2020s and beyond.)

Well-intentioned legislation designed to help one group can end up hurting not only that group but others as well. For example, in 2020, the state of California enacted a high-profile labor law (known as AB5) that focused on reclassifying hundreds of thousands of ride-sharing and delivery drivers as employees rather than independent contractors. The legislators thought this would help "gig" workers by making them eligible for health insurance, paid time off, and other benefits. This law was pushed through despite the fact that a significant number of the drivers enjoyed their independence — especially the freedom to create their own schedules. Most worrisome, and not fully foreseen, was that the law dragged many other gig workers into the reclassification net. These included freelance journalists, magicians, translators, comedians, programmers, designers, actors, and physical therapists. A lot of them lost work because many organizations found that implementing AB5's measures was too costly and decided to cut back on hiring their services.

And then there is the "Streisand Effect," the phenomenon in which an attempt to censor or hide information has the unintended consequence of publicizing that information more widely. Here is the background. In 2003, photographer Kenneth Adelman shot over 12,000 aerial pictures for the California Coastal Records Project, a group documenting soil erosion for the government. Included was a shot of the Malibu property of singer Barbra Streisand (it was labeled simply as "Image 3850"). Streisand caught wind of this project, claimed invasion of privacy, and filed suit to have it removed. Prior to Streisand's action, the photo had been downloaded a total of only six times. One month after her suit became public, the picture had been downloaded nearly a half a million times!

The Wise Fool believes that when things are made larger or their number is increased, they can take on a complex, new life of their own, and unexpected — even undesirable — things can happen. Here's how it works. Let's say that you have a recipe for strawberry shortcake that serves four people. One day you invite seven friends over to eat this dessert. To make it, you simply *double* the recipe's proportions. On another occasion, you invite one friend over for this dessert. To make it, all you do is *halve* the recipe's proportions.

Now suppose you invite 50,000 people over for strawberry shortcake. At this point, the biggest challenges confronting

you have nothing to do with the recipe: buying strawberries on the commodities market; making deals with the Teamsters to deliver enough cream; traffic coordination; and large-scale renting of chairs, tables, bowls, and spoons. The same things can happen when projects and ideas become bigger: issues come up that were not even imagined in the original plans.

A recent example of the "strawberry-shortcake" phenomenon is the increase in size of container ships in the first two decades of this century (a story that has been documented by economist Marc Levinson). In 2003, as the growth rate in world trade was kicking into high gear, the Danish shipping giant Maersk commissioned the construction of a new giant "Euromax" class of container ships that were 50% larger than anything currently in service. These behemoths were over four football fields long and were capable of transporting more than 12,000 TEUs of containers (industry lingo for *Twenty-foot Equivalent Units*, or enough containers for 6,000 fully loaded 40-foot trucks). Maersk made a bet that the growth in world trade would continue to be robust, and that their mammoth ships with increased carrying capacity would give the company an enormous competitive price advantage.

Of course, Maersk's rivals did not sit idly by. They commissioned large ships of their own, and a "giant ship arms race" was under way. Ten years later, in 2013, container ships that could carry 18,000 TEUs were in service, and ships capable of transporting 23,000 TEUs were on order.

Giantism soon spread to the ports. To accommodate these megaships, shipping terminals had to be expanded. This meant lengthening wharves, adding larger cranes (some as tall as 15-story buildings), and vastly increasing the area devoted to storing many thousands of additional containers. Other surrounding infrastructure also had to be modified: widened canals, deeper harbors, higher bridges, and refurbished roadways and railway heads. Within this huge staging ground, the process of unloading and loading containers took considerably longer compared to the smaller pre-2003 ships. As a result, these giant ships frequently left port behind schedule, making their customers unhappy.

As the growth rate of global shipping slackened in the late 2000s, many of the ships often left port only half-full. To save on fuel costs, the cargo companies reduced their ships' speed — throwing a monkey wrench into their customers' well-crafted "just-in-time" supply chains. The end result was that significantly more capacity was created than was necessary. The megaships proved to be a huge liability for Maersk, and by the mid-2010s Maersk had to sell off parts of itself to keep the company afloat. As Levinson put it: "Whether there was a need for a ship that could deliver 11,000 full-size truck loads was almost a second thought." But cautioning against the unexpected consequences of "more" is certainly something the Wise Fool would have been advocating had one been consulted.*

---

*The Maersk episode of "more" reminds me of a Buddhist tale told by Kakuaki Tanahashi. It seems that a man was invited by his neighbor for dinner. The man took a few bites of the meal but complained that he found the food "tasteless." The neighbor offered the man some salt. He proceeded to sprinkle it on his meal, and to his delight, he found the meal quite tasty. The man then reasoned: "If a small amount of salt improves the flavor, think of what a lot might do." He pushed his meal aside, and began to eat the salt by itself. Before long, he had burned his mouth and was writhing in pain.

Of course, I should mention that unintended consequences can also be positive, the most famous of which is the "invisible hand," a metaphor coined by the 18th-century Scottish economist Adam Smith. Smith held that each person, seeking only his own gain, "is led by an invisible hand to promote an end which was no part of his intention," which results in something positive for the public good. "It is not from the benevolence of the butcher, or the baker, that we expect our dinner," he said, "but from regard to their own self-interest."

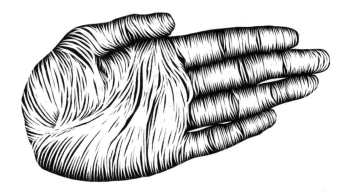

Sometimes ideas make weird and unexpected round-trips. Here's a fun example. In the early 2000s, video game makers such as Sony and EA Sports paid licensing fees to sports teams to record sound effects and crowd reactions from NBA, MLB, NFL, and European Soccer events for use in their sports video games. These included cheers, roars, saves, big plays, boos, and chants. These sounds were then cleaned up and organized into a sound library of different effects and reactions to be used at the appropriate time in the video game action.

During the 2020 coronavirus pandemic, many sporting

events prohibited spectators from attending. What to do about giving these events a sound of realism for the players on the field and the television audiences? Video game companies spotted an opportunity and sold this very same ballpark crowd noise back to teams. For example, Major League Baseball teams played crowd sounds from its official video game into empty ball parks to match what was happening on the field. Perhaps Adam Smith would say this is an example of the "invisible hand" at work!

Summary: The Wise Fool believes that sometimes the solution to a problem can make the situation worse than it was originally. Intervening in complex systems can create unanticipated and often undesirable outcomes. When you're evaluating ideas, try to imagine and anticipate the unintended consequences of our actions — especially the negative ones.

Wise Fool Strategy #19

Develop a
Thick Skin

"A thick skin is a gift from God."
— Konrad Adenauer, German Statesman

The Wise Fool knows that new ideas can be threatening, and they often provoke a negative reaction. For example, when Johannes Kepler correctly solved the orbital problem of the planets by using ellipses rather than circles, he was initially denounced by astronomers (and ignored by Galileo). When Ignaz Semmelweis proposed that doctors could reduce patient infections by frequently washing themselves with chlorinated lime water, he was reviled by his colleagues, who resented his implication that they were walking around with "death on their hands." When Igor Stravinsky first presented his *Rite of Spring* ballet with its unusual harmonies and primitive rhythms, he was met with a rioting audience.

Similarly, Wise Fools understand that their offbeat ideas can be viewed unfavorably and occasionally seen as menacing. Indeed, they realize that some people will respond to their insights with comments like "too strange," "contrary to policy," "impractical," or "makes no sense." Maybe the naysayers are right — sometimes the Wise Fool's ideas are half-baked. Remember, though, that people will often shoot these ideas down because either they feel threatened or they're too lazy to look for merit in them.

Wise Fools know that having a "thick skin" is essential for them to do their job. It means that they will not be easily offended, upset, or insulted by others' reactions. Indeed, a thick skin helps them to understand that *the only things that can affect them are the things that they allow to affect them.* American abolitionist Frederick Douglass had the right attitude to withstand the barbs and taunts hurled his way: "I prefer to be true to myself even at the hazard of incurring the ridicule of others, rather than be false, and to incur my own abhorrence."

The Wise Fool believes that if you are overly concerned with other people's opinions of you — that is, "thin-skinned" — then you will have difficulty expressing unusual viewpoints or making the offbeat remarks that fuel further discussion. The Wise Fool says it is a lot easier to present alternative ideas if you can emotionally shield yourself from other people's criticism, indifference, and scoffing laughter.

This "thick skin" mindset is captured in a delightful early scene in the film *Lawrence of Arabia*. In it, Lawrence lights a fellow soldier's cigarette and then nonchalantly watches the match burn all the way down as he holds it in his fingers. The other soldier observes this, tries the same feat, but burns his hand and screams: "Ow, that hurts. What's the trick?" To which Lawrence responds:

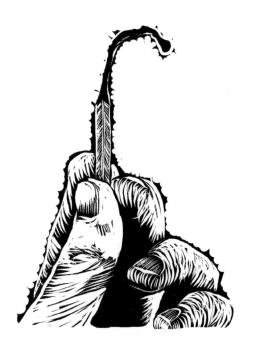

Certainly it hurts. The trick
is not minding that it hurts.

To paraphrase Lawrence, the trick to being "thick-skinned" is not minding the insults, silence, or criticism that come our way when we engage in Wise Fool behavior, and simply appreciating that they come with the territory.

Indeed, it can be quite liberating when you feel there will be few or no consequences resulting from what others think. This was the tack used by physicist Richard Feynman, who often said:

What do you care what
other people think?

He found that this prevented him from shaping his thinking around other people's interests and agendas.

Summary: Wise Fools know that when you do an inventory of your cognitive tool kit, it's as important to possess a "thick skin" as it is to have a wry wit, an ambiguous outlook, a sense of humility, a playful attitude, or a grasp of the obvious. They believe that if you are overly sensitive, you won't have the courage to approach the world in an offbeat way. They say, "What negative reaction do you expect? How can you deflect it, and not let it affect you emotionally?" They don't see opposing points of view as threats to their well-being. They never say (except perhaps in jest): "I am too sensitive for this — it might hurt my feelings."

Wise Fool Strategy #**20**

Shed an Illusion

"Shedding an illusion can make you wiser than discovering a new truth."

— Ludwig Börne, German Philosopher

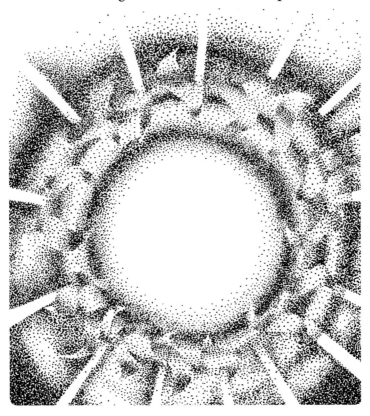

If the Wise Fool has a guiding belief from which much of his philosophy emanates, it would probably be something akin to this section's opening words from the 19th-century German philosopher Ludwig Börne. Indeed, all of the Strategies invite us to let go of one way of thinking and to seek out alternatives.

Wise Fools believe that it is their job to point out the things that we believe to be true but which are actually illusions. Or, as the American humorist Will Rogers put it in a more homespun way:

It isn't what we don't know that gives us trouble, it's what we do know that ain't so.

Wise Fools understand that it takes a degree of humility to discard an idea you once thought was beneficial but which is no longer valid. From this shedding, wisdom arises.

Here is the classic example of something humans believed to be true that turned out to be an illusion. From the beginning of civilization, one of humankind's most basic truths was that the sun revolves around the Earth. That this was true was easy to verify: a person could walk out his front door and confirm it with his own experience. Each day he would see the sun rise in the east, circle high overhead at noon, and then set later in the west. For millennia, this commonsense perception imposed itself on human consciousness as a truth.

This changed in the mid-16th century with the posthumous publication of an astronomical work by the Polish cleric Nicolaus Copernicus. Copernicus postulated that the sun's revolution around the earth was *merely an illusion created by the earth's own daily rotation on its own axis.* He further posited that it is the earth that revolves around the sun and not vice versa.

Though Copernicus's ideas were initially scoffed at, succeeding generations of scientists — including Galileo, Kepler, and Newton — found that shedding the illusion of geocentrism allowed them to question other apparent truths, reexamine past assumptions, reinterpret data, search for better explanations, and ultimately discover newer truths. The real enlightenment, however, came when people grasped that if a long-held truth could turn out to be an illusion, the same might also happen with any new discoveries they arrived at. This is quite an insight: every truth you discover can be ephemeral and ultimately proven to be illusory. Once again, this recognition should give us some humility about the robustness of our knowledge.

Indeed, the Wise Fool would argue that many of the truths we hold in life are illusory. A belief that was true at one part of our lives can become merely a chimera at another part, and should be shed. For example, when I was younger, these were a few of the beliefs that governed my outlook:

- By means of hard work and training, I could become a world-class competitive swimmer.

- The university provides the best setting to develop a "life of the mind."

- The government has people's best interests at heart.

- Experts should be heavily relied on for public policy decisions.

- A well-conceived, well-designed product will generally succeed in the marketplace.

Through lived experience, I came to realize that these notions were illusions (at least for me), and I shed them. This allowed me to discover more appropriate guiding ideas. This same process has repeated itself many times over the course of my life — especially with regard to my thoughts about family, parenting, relationships, politics, business, design, and matters of spirituality.

Perhaps Mark Twain had something like this in mind when he said:

One of life's most overvalued pleasures is sexual intercourse, and one of life's least appreciated is defecation.

Twain knew that there is something quite liberating about letting go of a previously cherished idea because it gives us the freedom to look for new ones.

Summary: The Wise Fool believes that we have many more misconceptions in our worldview than we would like to imagine. We should ask ourselves, "What is illusory in our outlook and can be shed? What conventional wisdom can we ignore?"

Part III:
Use Your Wise
Fool Know-How

**"The cleverest of all, in my opinion,
is the person who calls himself a fool
at least once a month."**

— Fyodor Dostoyevsky, Russian Novelist

1. Ask the Wise Fool Oracle

One of my favorite ways to use the Wise Fool Strategies is to consult them as an oracle. This gives me a "quick hit of inspiration." Let's take a moment to understand what an oracle does.

Over the millennia, many cultures have developed their own versions of this intuitive tool. Some examples: the ancient Chinese *I Ching*, the Egyptian *Tarot*, the Nordic *Runes*, the North American Indian *Medicine Wheel*, and the *Creative Whack Pack*. Perhaps you have benefited from using some (or all) of these tools.

Most oracles consist of a series of messages from which the questioner randomly selects one or several. The purpose of querying an oracle is not so much to foretell the future as it is to enable questioners to *delve more deeply into their own intuition when dealing with a problem*. Here is an example of some of the elements involved in consulting an oracle.

There once was an Indian medicine man whose job included creating hunting maps for his tribe. Whenever game got sparse, he would lay a piece of fresh leather out in the sun to dry. Then he would fold it and twist it in his hands, say a few prayers over it, and smooth it out.

The rawhide was now crisscrossed with lines and wrinkles. The medicine man marked some basic reference points on the rawhide, and — presto! — a new game map was created. The wrinkles represented new trails the hunters should follow. When the hunters followed the map's newly defined trails, they invariably discovered abundant game. Moral: By allow-

ing the rawhide's random folds to represent hunting trails, he pointed the hunters to places they had not previously looked.

In a similar fashion, I believe that we can use the Wise Fool Strategies as an oracle. Let's go through these simple steps one by one.

First: You need a specific question, topic, or issue on which you would like a fresh perspective. *(The medicine man wanted to find new places to find game.)* It could be a problem you're currently working on, or a decision you need to make. Clear your mind so that you are in a receptive state. Now formulate your question. For example:

"What should I focus on to gain understanding in my current situation?"

Second: You need an answer from the Wise Fool that addresses your question. *(The medicine man folded and twisted a piece of rawhide.)* This book contains 20 such answers — the Wise Fool Strategies. Open it at random to any page: the Strategy you pick is your answer.

Why use random Strategies? Since we tend to employ the same problem-solving approaches repeatedly, we usually come up with the same types of answers. Selecting a random Strategy forces us to look at our problems in ways we would not have done otherwise, and this can do wonders to stimulate our thinking.

You can also get a random number by googling "random number from 1 to 20." You might try asking Siri or Alexa for a random number. For example, if you select "10," then Strategy #10, "See the Obvious," is your answer. You then might turn to page 111 for more information.

(Rolling a D20 role-playing die also works nicely — it's the icosahedron-shaped one. Speaking of icosasahedra, use the template on the next page to create your very own Wise Fool icosahedron. Simply copy it and then fold it into the 20-sided shape.)

Third: Ask yourself how the Strategy you picked relates to your question. *(The medicine man interpreted the folded lines to be hunting trails.)* Imagine that it is the Wise Fool giving you counsel. What sense can you make out of it?

11 Use Your Forgettery

13 Kiss A Favorite Idea Goodbye

15 Find What's out of Whack

5 Keep Playing with it

18 Imagine the Unintended

4 Seek Other Right Answers

12 Drop What's Obsolete

2 Flex Your Risk Muscle

20 Shed An Illusion

14 Revisit a Discarded Idea

10 See the Obvious

8 Build on an Odd Idea

16 Stop Fooling Yourself

6 Reverse Your Perspective

17 Exercise Humility

3 Laugh At It

19 Develop A Thick Skin

9 Look for Ambiguity

7 Fool Around with the Constraints

1 Buck the Crowd

Fool @ WiseFool.net

Try to think of as many different contexts as possible in which the Strategy has meaning. Don't worry about how practical or logical you are. What's important is to give free rein to your imagination. If you need some mental lubricant to get things moving, I recommend reading my commentary for that particular Strategy.

Each Wise Fool Strategy is sufficiently flexible (and ambiguous) so that it can be applied to a wide range of contexts and situations. Thus, no matter which stage of the creative process you're in, each of the Strategies can speak to you. For example, "Seek Other Right Answers" (#4):

- If you're looking for information, this Strategy tells you to go beyond the first right answer you find and to seek out others.

- If you're playing around with ideas, it advises you to put them in unusual contexts to give them new meanings.

- If you're evaluating concepts, it reminds you to keep an open mind, and *not* to fall in love with one specific decision-making criterion.

- If you're implementing ideas, it tells you to be flexible with your game plan and tactics.

Most Wise Fool Strategies will trigger an immediate response. Sometimes, however, you'll look at one and think, "This has nothing to do with my question," and be tempted to dismiss it. Don't! Force yourself to make a connection. Often those ideas that initially seem the least relevant turn out to be the most important because they point to something that you've been completely overlooking.

Thus, if "Laugh at It" (#3) isn't the usual thing you think of when dealing with a problem, then your reflections on this Strategy are likely to give you a new take on your question.

For example, during the course of writing this book, I got stuck on a passage introducing the Wise Fool. I drew "Kiss a Favorite Idea Goodbye" (#13), and quickly realized my thinking had been blocked because I had become infatuated with a particular story about Wise Fool behavior. It was an amusing story, but the Strategy helped me to understand that it halted the flow of the narrative and didn't belong. I jettisoned it, and my writing proceeded smoothly.

Recently, my wife was trying to resolve a scheduling conflict with one of her relatives. She consulted the Wise Fool and picked "Develop a Thick Skin" (#19). She opted to give herself a license to rededicate herself to what she thought was the appropriate action and to be less concerned with any criticism.

One time my message was "Use Your Forgettery" (#11). I decided to work on a different project that day. Later, I returned to my original project with a clearer perspective and made much progress.

When is the best time to move on and ask the Wise Fool for another answer? When you're done with the current answer. That could be in two minutes, two hours—or in two days.

Variation: This is similar to the procedure just outlined, but here you select *two random Strategies* instead of one. When you do this, you'll find that each Strategy provides a context for the other and allows you to think more specifically about your question.

Drawing "Flex Your Risk Muscle" (#2) and "Fool Around with the Constraints" (#7) might mean: aggressively challenge the rules governing your issue, and even slay a few of its sacred cows.

"Exercise Humility" (#17) and "Buck the Crowd" (#1) could mean: leave the comfort of the group, and have the humility of "beginner's mind" to take a different path.

"Stop Fooling Yourself" (#16) and "Seek Other Right Answers" (#4): you are deceiving yourself if you think that you've correctly figured out what the problem is, and you should look for additional ways your issue could be defined.

"Develop a Thick Skin" (#19) and "Reverse Your Perspective" (#6) could mean: break a major routine that relates to the issue, and be less concerned about any discomfort that might arise.

2. The Strategies as Daily Mantras

Another way to use the Wise Fool Strategies is as a daily *mantra*. What's a mantra? It's a Sanskrit term, and traditionally it referred to a word or phrase a person chanted during meditation (usually within a Hindu or Buddhist religious context).

In recent decades, however, the word "mantra" has taken on a broader, more secular meaning. It has become a kind of motto or slogan that encapsulates a person's philosophy on the proper way to approach a specific activity (and be successful at it). Invoking a mantra can help you get into the right state of mind to reach your goal for a specific task.*

To think like a Wise Fool, simply select a Strategy in the morning, and have it be your "mantra of the day." You then look for opportunities to apply it as the day unfolds.

If you picked "Develop a Thick Skin" (#19), you might make a point of sticking your neck out during the day, and be less concerned about any personal discomfort or criticism that might result.

Suppose you chose "Laugh at It" (#3). You would then make an extra effort to view the incongruous things you encounter during the day with a sense of lightness, amusement, and good humor. If you were in a meeting where the other people were too serious, you might give yourself permission to ask a question that injected some irreverence into the situation. If you saw something that was a bit awkward, you might laugh at it and make a series of jokes. (If you wanted to make a game out of it, you could tie in George Bernard Shaw's belief, "When a thing is funny, search for a hidden truth." Who knows, maybe

---

* Here are a few examples:
- "Less is more." [For a designer]
- "A dull knife is more dangerous than a sharp one." [For a chef]
- "Sail away from the safe harbor." [For a risk-taker]
- "Always code as if the guy who ends up maintaining your code will be a psychopath who knows where you live." [For a programmer]

you would have a list of deep insights at the end of the day!)

Taking "Reverse Your Perspective" (#6) would provide you with a license for doing things differently: use your non-dominant hand for brushing your teeth and combing your hair, take a different means of transportation to work, eat your dessert before the entrée, and so on.

Picking "Exercise Humility" (#17) might allow you to adopt a nonjudgmental frame of mind as you go about your day and perform your various tasks.

Selecting "Build on an Odd Idea" (#8) would allow you to conjure up unusual thoughts: What if all high school biology students had their own cadavers to work on? They'd get to know a person inside out. They would also learn the importance of taking good care of themselves firsthand.

Choosing "Find What's out of Whack" (#15) would give you a daylong opportunity to activate your "crap detector." You could start by examining your own core values and determine whether you are living up to them in your actions. You could also apply this Strategy to all the people and things you see that promise one thing but which actually cause something else to happen: politicians, media organizations, advertisements, and poorly designed products, to name but a few.

At the end of each day, reflect back on how often you were able to "activate" the message in the Strategy you selected as your "thought for the day." I think you'll find that using the Wise Fool Strategies as daily mantras is a good way to help you incorporate them into your thinking.

3. Have Fun!

To develop your ability to think like a Wise Fool, I highly recommend consulting the Strategies on a regular basis. Not only will they provoke different and original thoughts each time you consult them, they will become valued companions whose guidance you will welcome!

4. Final Thoughts

If we were to ask a veteran Wise Fool to share some of the basics of Wise Fool thinking, it would go something like this:

"You need other people for their ideas, stimulation, and suggestions, but if you're agreeing with them most of the time, you are not doing your own thinking.

"It takes nerve to stand out from the crowd, to ask the odd questions, and to propose unpopular ideas. This is especially important when there is a topic others are afraid to discuss — the proverbial 'elephant in the room.' On occasions such as this, courage is a good quality to possess.

"Looking for the humor in a situation is a surefire way to refresh your mind. Relax your 'stupid monitor' and make fun of your basic beliefs and assumptions. There's nothing quite like a bit of irreverence to help you loosen up and put yourself in a mood more conducive to seeing alternatives.

"There are very few things so serious that a little lightheartedness and whimsy can't improve. Indeed, the world likes it when you chuckle at its incongruities, inconsistencies, and general weirdness.

"Stay curious. Be the one who is continually asking 'why?' Others may sometimes regard you as a smartass or a pain-in-the-butt, but persistent questioning is a hallmark of Wise Fool thinking.

"If an obstacle prevents you from moving forward, use it as an opportunity to try something different. Knowledge is the stuff from which new ideas are made, but forgetting what you know at the right time can also lead to surprising insights.

"Nothing evades your attention quite so persistently as that which you take for granted. See the obvious and find the good ideas right in front of you. Also notice the things that should be present or should be happening but *aren't*.

"Play is one of the best mental lubricants around. When you're fooling around with a problem, you have little concern about being practical or failing. Try removing a constraint or two . . . or better yet, add some as a way to move beyond conventional solutions. Also, most things can be improved by making them more fun to do.

"Reality is ambiguous. The color green represents 'low-lying land areas' on physical geography maps, 'argon' on gas canister labels, and 'paradise' in Tantra Yoga. Likewise, the situations we encounter can be interpreted in a variety of ways, depending on the contexts in which we think about them. This ambiguity gives us creative freedom.

"The second attempt on the same problem should come from a totally different direction. Studying the problem that is the opposite of the one you're facing will also provide you with a fresh perspective. Doing things in the reverse way from your customary method will allow you to discover the possibilities that are usually hidden.

"Any strategy that leads to success can ultimately lead to failure or stagnation. Thus, there are times when, in order to grow, you may have to let go of the very things that helped you prosper and attain success in the first place. Thinking differently means not only generating new ideas, it also means eliminating obsolete ones. Avoid falling in love with ideas; these can be the most difficult ones to let go of.

"You know less than you think you do. Watch out for the lies you tell yourself—self-deception is part and parcel of being alive. Being aware of your cognitive blind spots, perceptual constraints, and social biases can help you make better decisions.

"Check to see how your ego is adversely affecting your performance. Self-confidence — especially if it's based on past achievements—is laudable, but if it leads to an arrogant outlook, you could be setting yourself up for failure. A humble attitude is a wonderful tool for seeking out other solutions.

"The cosmos is an unpredictable place. Unexpected and unintended things happen. You never know where your just-conceived solution will lead you. Or what problems it might create.

"You learn something new every day. Make part of that learning shedding an illusion of something you formerly thought was true.

"And one more thing. There is more than one way to think like a Wise Fool. Figure out your own Wise Fool Strategies, and share them with others in your interactions with them! Discover the many situations where you can engage in this type of thinking and make a positive impact."

Remember, you've got abundant Wise Fool know-how. Use it to:

Be a creative contrarian!

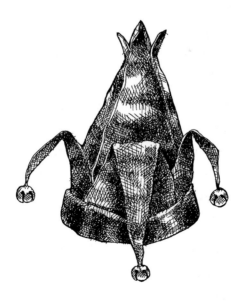

Selected Bibliography

Edwin Abbott. *Flatland: A Romance of Many Dimensions*. London: 1884.

W. Brian Arthur. *The Nature of Technology: What It Is and How It Evolves*. New York: Free Press, 2009.

Johann Sebastian Bach. *The Goldberg Variations*. Performed by Glenn Gould. New York: Columbia Records, 1956 and 1982.

Sebastian Brant. *The Ship of Fools*. Basel: 1494.

Martin Buber. *I and Thou*. Translated by Walter Kaufmann. New York, Scribners, 1970.

Lewis Carroll. *Alice In Wonderland*. London: 1865.

Ernst Cassirer. *The Philosophy of Symbolic Forms*. 3 volumes. New Haven: Yale University Press, 1953–1957.

Ron Chernow. *Titan: The Life of John D. Rockefeller, Sr.* New York: Random House, 1998.

Paul Ciotti. *More with Less: Paul MacCready and the Dream of Efficient Flight*. San Francisco: Encounter, 2002

Mark Dunn. *Ella Minnow Pea*. San Francisco: MacAdam Cage, 2001.

Desiderius Erasmus. *In Praise of Folly*. Rotterdam: 1511.

Richard Feynman. *"Surely You're Joking, Mr. Feynman!": Adventures of a Curious Character*. New York: Norton, 1985. [I have a Corgi named "Shirley You're Joking."]

James Gleick. *The Information: A History, a Theory, a Flood*. New York: Random House, 2011.

Heraclitus. *Fragments*. Commentary and Translation by T.M. Robinson. Toronto: University of Tornoton Press, 1987.

Charma Halpern. Del Close, *Truth in Comedy: The Manual of Improvisation*. Denver: Merriweather Publishing, 1994.

Christopher Hitchens. *Letters to a Young Contrarian*. New York: Basic Books, 2001.

Henry Hobhouse. *The Seeds of Change: Five Plants That Transformed Mankind.* New York: Harper Collins, 1987.

Jamie Holmes. *Nonsense: The Power of Not Knowing.* New York: Crown, 2015.

I Ching. Translated by Richard Wilhelm: Princeton, 1950.

Daniel Kahneman. *Thinking, Fast and Slow.* New York: Farrar, Straus and Giroux, 2011.

Immanuel Kant. *Critique of Pure Reason.* Riga: Johann Friedrich Hartknoch, 1781.

Arthur Koestler. *The Act of Creation.* New York: MacMillan, 1964.

Lao Tzu. *Tao Te Ching.* Translated by Stephen Mitchell. New York: Harper, 2006.

Leonard Koren. *Wabi Sabi: For Artists, Designers, Poets, Philosophers.* Berkeley: Stone Bridge Press, 1994.

Milan Kundera. *The Book of Laughter and Forgetting.* New York, Knopf, 1980.

Marc Levinson. *Outside the Box: How Globalization Changed from Moving Stuff to Spreading Ideas.* Princeton, Princeton University Press, 2020.

Mario Livio. *The Golden Ratio: The Story of Phi, the World's Most Astonishing Number.* New York: Broadway, 2002.

Katie Mack. *The End of Everything (Astrophysically Speaking).* New York: Scribner, 2020.

Gustav Mahler. *Symphony #4 in G Major.* The New York Philharmonic Orchestra, conducted by Leonard Bernstein; Reri Grist, Soprano. New York: Columbia Records, 1960.

Ken McNab. *And in the End: The Last Days of the Beatles.* New York: Thomas Dunne, 2019.

Humphrey P. Neill. *The Art of Contrary Thinking.* (5th ed.) Caldwell, ID: Caxton Press, 1985.

Wes "Scoop" Nesker. *The Essential Crazy Wisdom: The Saint, the Zen Master, the Poet, the Fool*. Berkeley: Ten Speed Press, 2001.

George Orwell. *1984*. London: Secker & Warburg, 1949.

Plato. *The Apology of Socrates*. [4th cent. BC]

Plutarch. *Lives of the Noble Greeks and Romans*. [2nd cent. AD]

William Shakespeare. *King Lear*. London: 1606.

S. Subramanian. *A Dominant Character: The Radical Science and Restless Politics of J.B.S. Haldane*. New York: Norton, 2020.

James Surowiecki. *The Wisdom of Crowds: Why the Many Are Smarter Than the Few*. New York: Doubleday, 2004.

Nassim Nicholas Taleb. *The Black Swan: The Impact of the Highly Improbable*. New York: Random House, 2007.

Kazuaki Tanahashi. *A Flock of Fools: Ancient Buddhist Tales of Wisdom and Laughter*. New York: Grove Press, 2004.

Thucydides. *History of the Peloponnesian War*. [5th cent. BC]

Robert Trivers. *The Folly of Fools: The Logic of Deceit and Self-Deception in Human Life*. New York: Basic Books, 2011.

Mark Twain. *Adventures of Huckleberry Finn*. New York: 1884.

Kurt Vonnegut. *Cat's Cradle*. New York: Holt, Rinehart, and Winston, 1963.

Roger von Oech. *A Whack on the Side of the Head: How You Can Be More Creative*. (4th ed.) New York: Hachette, 2008.

Roger von Oech. *Expect the Unexpected: A Creativity Tool Based on the Ancient Wisdom of Heraclitus*. New York: Free Press, 2001.

Paul Watzlawick. *How Real Is Real? Confusion, Disinformation, and Communication*. New York: Random House, 1976.

William Willeford. *The Fool and His Sceptre: A Study in Clowns and Jesters*. London: Edward Arnold, 1969.

Christopher Williams. *Origins of Form: The Shape of Natural and Man-Made Things*. New York: Architectural Group, 1981.

Index of Proper Names

Ansel Adams 95
Kenneth Adelman 163
Konrad Adenauer 169
Alexander the Great 92, 155
Saul Alinsky 54
Peter Allen 135
St. Ambrose 28
Hans Christian Andersen 41
Aristophanes 142
Aristotle 6
Solomon Asch 38
St. Augustine 28
Bingo Barnes iii
Count Basie 61
Norman D. Beachhead 89
The Beatles 33, 89
Bellamy Brothers 104
Tom Berenger 149
John Betjeman 47
Niels Bohr 15, 53
Napoleon Bonaparte 126, 153
Bob Bowman 86
Ludwig Börne 173
Sebastian Brant 137
Georges Braque 78
Giordano Bruno 138
Martin Buber 157
Guatama Buddha 134
Simcha Bunin 157
David Burge 58
Ray Charles 93
Émile-Auguste Chartier 59
Ron Chernow 162
César Cielo 116
Paul Ciotti 119
Christopher Columbus 119

Confucius 156
Nicolaus Copernicus 42, 174
Hernán Cortés 35
Francis Crick 79
Croesus of Lydia 108
Nicholas of Cusa 137
Cyrus the Great 108
Dante Alighieri 142
Charles Darwin 74, 143
Roger Deakins 96
Philip Dhingra 113
Walt Disney 56
Frederick Douglass 170
Fyodor Dostoyevsky 177
Peter Drucker 125
Mark Dunn 97
Bob Dylan 89
Albert Einstein 94
Dwight D. Eisenhower 89
Desiderius Erasmus 137
Arthur Erickson 120
Till Eulenspiegel 35
Joel Fagliano 89
William Faulkner 131
Adriana Ferrarese 158
Richard Feynman 79, 147, 172
Jack Finney 29
Rudolph Flesch 130
Henry Ford 133
Rosalind Franklin 79
Frederick the Great 126
Sigmund Freud 101
Milton Friedman 63
Allen Funt 26
Galileo Galilei 170, 175
Murray Gell-Mann 78

Edward Gibbon 72
Giotto di Bondone 93
James Gleick 78
Jean-Luc Godard 72
Jeff Goldblum 149
Julann Griffin 82
Merv Griffin 82
Brothers Grimm 146
Johannes Gutenberg 74
Joseph Heller 142
Jimi Hendrix 89
Heraclitus 121, 155
Heinrich Himmler 48
Thomas Hirschfield 128
Christopher Hitchens 36
Adolf Hitler 155
Henry Hobson 67
Billie Holiday 93
Eugène Ionesco 13
Jesus of Nazareth 141
Penn Jillette 148
Steve Jobs 6
James Joyce 70, 78
Lawrence Kasdan 149
Johannes Kepler 42, 170, 175
Jack Kerouac 47
Arthur Koestler 37
Henry Kremer 119
Stanley Kubrick 142
Milan Kundera 103
Akira Kurosawa 64
Jean-Baptiste Lamarck 143
Lao Tzu 49
T.S. Lawrence 171
Vladimir Lenin 144
Pope Leo X 44

Marc Levinson 165
Lin Chi 134
Louis XIV 101
Eric Lumer 78
Martin Luther 44
Trofim Lysenko 143
Paul MacCready 119
Niccolò Machiavelli 5
Charles Mackay 33
Roger Martin du Gard 133
Karl Marx 143
Abraham Maslow 61
Ken McNab 34
Philipp Melanchthon 138
H.L. Mencken 58
Gregor Mendel 143
Andrea Mercer 81
King Midas 160
Henry Miller 117
John Milton 72
Billy Mitchell 44
John Montague 140
Michel de Montaigne 138
Thomas More 137
Samuel Morse 77
Wolfgang Amadeus Mozart 158
Elon Musk 94
Richard Narramore 199
Nero 68
Isaac Newton 94
Friedrich Nietzsche 57
Edwin Nourse 32
William of Ockham 54
David Ogilvy 57
George Orwell 45, 116, 142
Dorothy Parker 139

George S. Patton 89
St. Paul 1
Tom Peters 150
Michael Phelps 86
Pablo Picasso 78
Charle Piccirillo 71
Pico della Mirandola 137
Plato 42
Plutarch 92
Amy Poehler 100
Lorenzo Da Ponte 158
Neil Postman 83, 152
Pythagoras 122
Paul Rand 133
James Reeves 116
Joan Rivers 39, 140
John D. Rockefeller 161
John Rodefer 46
Will Rogers 174
Theodore Roosevelt 161
Vera Rubin 94
Jalai ad-Din Rumi 77, 111
Sappho 94
Artur Schnabel 76
Ignaz Semmelweis 170
Seneca 158
Rod Serling 109
Idries Shah 61
William Shakespeare 9, 72
George Bernard Shaw 185
Shirley You're Joking 193
Will Shortz 89
Don Siegel 29
Frank Sinatra 93
Upton Sinclair 45
Alfred Sloan 31
Adam Smith 167

Socrates 7, 156
Stephen Sondheim 96
Joseph Stalin 143
Ringo Starr 34
Igor Stravinsky 170
Barbra Streisand 164
Albert Szent-Györgyi 2
Sun Tzu 88
Nassim Nicholas Taleb 157
Kakuaki Tanahashi 166
Ian Tattersal 159
(Raymond) Teller 148
John Templeton 33
Rick Tendy 122
Robert Trivers 149
Mark Twain 25, 72, 142, 176
Duchess of Tyrol 87
Alfred Vail 77
Charles Van Doren 82
Nikolai Vavilov 144
Voltaire 142
Florian von Donnersmarck 155
Kurt Vonnegut 13, 69
John von Neumann 78
Wendy von Oech 183
Abraham Wald 115
David Foster Wallace 112
James Watson 79
Thomas Watson Jr. 3
Bill Watterson 71
Paul Watzlawick 87, 151
Oscar Wilde 48
John Wilkes 140
Christopher Williams 123
Ludwig Wittgenstein 13, 58
Frank Lloyd Wright 91
Xerxes of Persia 108

Acknowledgments

I'd like to thank Richard Narramore, my editor at Wiley, for his invaluable assistance in shaping and promoting this work. It was a pleasure kicking ideas around with him. I also appreciate the efforts from Deborah Schindlar, Donna J. Weinson, Paul McCarthy, Jessica Filippo, and Victoria Anllo to make this book a reality.

Thanks to illustrator Mark "Bingo" Barnes for his drawings: they add a fun dimension to this work.

I'm also grateful to the following for their assistance along the way: Stuart Kaplan, Bobbie Bensaid, Ricardo Cruz, and Paula Palmer at U.S. Games for their championing of Wise Fool ideas; Rick Wolfe, Beth deGuzman, and Dan Ambrosio at Hachette; and, finally, 3D designers Jason and Zach Hilbourne, new media savant David Armano, business mentor Wiley Caldwell, Ethernet inventor Bob Metcalfe, video game pioneer Nolan Bushnell, world-class toy expert Peter Craig, AI wizard Philip Dhingra, novelist Katherine Seligman, publishing legend Bill Shinker, and artist George Willett for their many-decades long support of my projects.

I appreciate Alex von Oech, Jodi von Oech, Athena von Oech, Andrew Maisel, and Heather Gamper for sharing their ideas with me about this book.

And, finally, many thanks to Wendy, my wife and lifelong muse, for her contributions. *The Creative Contrarian* would not have happened without her insights and guidance.

About the Author

Roger von Oech has spent a lifetime listening to his own Wise Fool. He started his company, Creative Think, in 1977 to stimulate innovation in business through seminars, conferences, publications, and software. His presentations and products have enhanced the creativity of many millions around the world. His clients have ranged from Apple, IBM, Cartier, Nestlé, and Disney to Coca-Cola, NASA, Google, Microsoft, Sony, and USA Swimming.

He is the author of four books on creativity, including the classic *A Whack on the Side of the Head* (translated into 25 languages). He's also the creator of the *Creative Whack Pack* card deck and iOS app. In addition, he is the inventor of a line of magnetic manipulative geometrical toys, the most popular of which is the *Ball of Whacks*.

He is a *Phi Beta Kappa* graduate of Ohio State University, and earned his Ph.D. from Stanford University in a self-conceived program in the "History of Ideas."

He is the father of two grown children, a grandfather of four, and lives with his wife, Wendy, in the Santa Cruz Mountains near Palo Alto, California.

*   *   *

I hope you enjoyed this work and got some ideas from reading it. If you have any comments or stories you'd like to share, I'd love to see them. Please send them to:

fool@wisefool.net